D1307645

THE LEGEND OF

Litton

INDUSTRIES

THE LEGEND OF

Litton

INDUSTRIES

JEFFREY L. RODENGEN

Edited by Melody Maysonet
Design and layout by Sandy Cruz and Wendy Iverson

Also by Jeff Rodengen

The Legend of Chris-Craft

IRON FIST: The Lives
of Carl Kiekhaefer

Evinrude-Johnson and
The Legend of OMC

Serving the Silent Service:
The Legend of Electric Boat

The Legend of Dr Pepper/Seven-Up

The Legend of Honeywell

The Legend of Briggs & Stratton

The Legend of Ingersoll-Rand

The MicroAge Way

The Legend of Halliburton

The Legend of Stanley:
150 Years of The Stanley Works

The Legend of
York International

The Legend of Nucor Corporation

The Legend of Goodyear:
The First 100 Years

The Legend of AMP

The Legend of Cessna

The Legend of VF Corporation

The Spirit of AMD

New Horizons:
The Story of Ashland Inc

The Legend of Rowan

The History of American Standard

The Legend of Mercury Marine

The Legend of Federal-Mogul

Against the Odds:
Inter-Tel—The First 30 Years

The Legend of Pfizer

State of the Heart: The Practical Guide
to Your Heart and Heart Surgery
with Larry W. Stephenson, M.D.

The Legend of Worthington Industries

The Legend of Trinity Industries

The Legend of IBP

The Legend of
Cornelius Vanderbilt Whitney

Publisher's Cataloging in Publication

Rodengen, Jeffrey L.
  The legend of Litton Industries /Jeffrey L. Rodengen. —
1st ed.
   p. cm.
   Includes bibliographical references and index.
   ISBN 0-945903-51-0

  1. Litton industries. 2. defense industries — United States.
I. Title.

HD9743.U64L58 1999   388.4'7355'0973
           QBI98-1595

Copyright © 2000 by Write Stuff Enterprises, Inc. All rights reserved. No part of this book may be reproduced or transmitted in any form by any means, electronic or mechanical, including photocopying and recording, or by any information storage or retrieval system, without permission in writing from the publisher.

Write Stuff Enterprises, Inc.
1001 South Andrews Avenue, Second Floor • Fort Lauderdale, FL 33316
1-800-900-Book (1-800-900-2665) • (954) 462-6657
www.writestuffbooks.com

Library of Congress Catalog Card Number 99-61060
ISBN 0-945903-51-0

Completely produced in the United States of America
10 9 8 7 6 5 4 3 2 1

TABLE OF CONTENTS

FOREWORD

by
Senator Trent Lott
U.S. Senate Majority Leader

I WAS ONLY ONE YEAR OLD when my father went to work in Pascagoula, Mississippi, as a security guard at the Ingalls Shipyard (now the Ingalls Shipbuilding division of Litton Industries). He had followed his brother there, who, after completing a pharmacy course, had left the shipyard to run the drugstore at the shipyard gate. My father took some additional training at the yard and became a pipe fitter during the latter part of World War II. Near the end of the war, the shipbuilding was beginning to drop off, and my dad was drafted. He passed all his tests and was prepared to go overseas, but then the fighting ended. He had spent the entire war working in the shipyard.

My mother spent the war teaching first and second grades at Beach Elementary School in Pascagoula. In those busy wartime years, there were so many families who had come to work at the shipyard that the school ran two shifts, one for children of the morning shift workers and one for children of the afternoon shift.

After the war ended, we moved to northern Mississippi but returned to Pascagoula and to Ingalls about 1951. My dad started working on the high overhead cranes in the yard, but he couldn't get used to the height and returned to pipe fitting, both in the ships and in the pipe shop where subassemblies are fabricated. He continued to work intermittently at the shipyard until 1968, when he was killed in an automobile accident.

We lived in a mobile home a few blocks from the shipyard, so I grew up literally in the shadow of that yard. In high school, my future wife, Tricia, and I both played in the Pascagoula High School band. She played flute, and I played tuba, and we played patriotic songs at the christening of every ship that slid down the ways. Litton now has a more controlled launching system, but there was nothing like seeing thousands of tons of steel racing down those greased boards and splashing dramatically into the water.

Litton's timing was impeccable for acquiring Ingalls Shipbuilding Corporation in 1961. Having been in operation since 1938, Ingalls had built more than 250 ships, including more than 200 for the U.S. Navy. But the yard was experiencing financial difficulties, and as *Fortune* noted, shipbuilding in the United States was regarded as "a tired industry in a highly competitive world market."

Litton helped rejuvenate that tired industry. Overnight, the Ingalls acquisition made Litton the nation's third largest shipbuilder. The yard would eventually build a wide variety of ships, including nuclear submarines and sub-hunting surface warships such as destroyers and frigates. Litton was able to foresee the synergies Ingalls would have with its other divisions, for Litton's proprietary computers, fire-control systems and sonar and inertial guidance systems were destined for installation in these state-of-the-art ships.

I graduated from law school the year before my father died, and I went to work for Bill Colmer, the congressman from the Fifth Congressional District, which included Pascagoula. From that day, I started looking after Ingalls — not as somebody who depended on the shipyard, but on behalf of the congressman and on behalf of my friends, classmates and neighbors in Pascagoula.

Then, in 1970, with the support of Senator John Stennis and Congressman Colmer, who was on the Senate Armed Services Committee, Ingalls was awarded one of the largest ship construction contracts in history to produce 30 Spruance-class destroyers. Thirty in a single package! Armed with guided missiles, guns and antisubmarine weaponry, these multimission ships also carry helicopters to extend the fleet's defense and attack capability.

In 1972, at the tender age of 31, I was elected to Congress to succeed Bill Colmer from the same Fifth District that includes Pascagoula. It was a monumental time for me, sitting on the Judiciary Committee impeachment hearings of Richard Nixon and looking after the Ingalls shipyard.

To this day, I still run into people who knew my dad at the shipyard. I met one older gentleman, a pipe fitter, who worked at the yard as a young man and was my dad's helper. Over the years, of course, I've been very close to the shipyard and have been very proud of the work that's done there. It has been wonderful to see the diversity of work the yard has attracted, from cruise ships to container ships to ships for Israel and work for the Venezuelan navy. After the Spruance-class destroyers, Ingalls built the Kidd-class destroyers, followed by the Aegis-class cruisers, the Ticonderoga-class, and now the Aegis destroyers. Along the way, Ingalls built the LHA, multipurpose, amphibious ships for the Marines, along with their successors, the LHD, which are the biggest ships ever built at the yard.

Just last year, Congress provided the first phase of funds ($375 million) for the next generation of LHD — the LHD-8. I was surprised to have received very critical press from the national media that I was generating funds for my hometown of Pascagoula by promoting ships the Marine Corps supposedly didn't even want. First, I don't know why anyone would be criticized for doing the best he could for a major industry in his state — the biggest employer in the state of Mississippi. More significantly, this is a ship that the Marine Corps wanted and needed. In fact, I had handwritten notes from two commandants making the case that this ship was very important to the Marine Corps's future.

Another great source of pride for me is the extremely high quality of work that is done at Litton's Ingalls shipyard. The company was the first in the nation to develop a systematized modular approach to construction, which led to greater efficiency, not only at Ingalls, but at the other shipbuilding yards in our country and abroad. What I find most amazing, though, is that every ship Ingalls has produced since the early seventies — going all the way back to the Spruance-class ships — has been built under budget and ahead of schedule. Every ship. That is a tremendous compliment to the men and women of Litton at Ingalls.

My life, since I was one year old, has been inextricably intertwined with the men and women of that shipyard. Even today, it always surprises me when I go to the shipyard gates on election days just how many workers I know from junior high, high school and my many experiences over the years. I still have a lot of very good friends there, and they don't seem to mind the fact that I look after Ingalls every day.

U.S. Senator Trent Lott of Mississippi is the Senate's 16th Majority Leader. He was elected to the House of Representatives in 1972 and served until 1988, when he was elected to the Senate. After being elected for a second term in 1994, he became Majority Leader in 1996.

ACKNOWLEDGMENTS

A GREAT NUMBER OF PEOple assisted in the research, preparation and publication of *The Legend of Litton Industries.*

The principal research was accomplished by my talented and enterprising research assistant Bob Wisehart.

This work would not have been possible without generous assistance from many Litton executives, employees and retirees. I am indebted to Larry Ailinger, TASC; Larry Ball, president of Litton Poly-Scientific; Allan Baron, vice president, Advanced Technology; Darwin Beckel, corporate vice president and president of Guidance & Control; Randy Belote, Litton Media Relations; Arthur Bentley, former manager of executive communications and corporate publications; Allen Bernardini, president of Winchester Electronics and VEAM; Pierro Biagetti, president of Litton Italia; Henry Bodurka, retired president of Litton Enterprise Solutions; Jass Brasher, vice president for quality assurance at Ingalls Shipbuilding; Michael Brown, chairman, president and chief executive officer; Joseph Caligiuri, retired senior vice president; Kelly Coffield, president of Litton Life Support; Kitty Coleman, public relations liaison, Litton Network Access Systems; Jim Cox, vice president and chief financial officer of Ingalls Shipbuilding; Spencer Davis, corporate vice president for corporate communications and investor relations; Robert Del Boca, president of Laser Systems; George Fenimore, retired senior vice president and corporate secretary; Larry Frame, senior vice president and group executive for Advanced Electronics; James Frey, corporate vice president, strategic business development and president of TASC; Nancy Gaymon, corporate vice president, Human Resources; Richard George, retired chief technology officer, Data Systems Division; Michael Gering, president of Amecom; Harry Halamandaris, corporate executive vice president and chief operating officer for Electronics and Information Systems; Richard Hopman, corporate vice president and managing director of LITEF and TELDIX; Tom Hutchings, Litton chief technology officer; Una Vere Katter, advertising manager for Litton Data Systems; Robert Knapp, retired director of public relations; Den Knecht, vice president of Ingalls Shipbuilding; L.D. "Vern" Kramer, president of Kester Solder; Steven Lambert, president of Electro-Optical Systems; John Leonis, retired chairman and CEO; Donald Lepore, corporate senior vice president and group executive for Electronic Components and Materials; Robert Lentz, former board member; Frank Marshall, Jr., corporate vice president and associate general counsel; Steven Mazzo, president of Applied Technology; Glen McDaniel, retired corporate vice president and general counsel; Denny McSweeny, director, investor relations; David Miller, president of Airtron; Alden Munson, corporate senior vice president and group executive for Information Systems; Timothy Paulson, corporate vice president and treasurer; Leonard Pomata, corporate vice president and president of PRC; John Preston, corporate senior vice president and general counsel; Steve Ruh, senior photographer at Ingalls Shipbuilding; Beatrice Sargeant, retired administrative assistant to the president, Electron Devices Division; Bob Schutz, president of Advanced Circuitry and Inter-Pak Electronics; Gerald St. Pé, corporate executive vice president and chief operating officer for Litton Ship Systems; Bob Sterrett, marketing manager, Litton Poly-Scientific; D. Michael Steuert, corporate senior vice president and chief financial officer; Louis Tabor, president of Litton Network Access Systems; Jeanette Thomas, corporate vice president and secretary; Dr. Richard True, chief scientist, Electron Devices Division; Frank Tullis, vice president of business development at Litton Data Systems; Timothy Westover, president of Litton Systems Canada; Michael Worstell, vice president of contracts, Aero Products; and David Wright, vice president of Ingalls Shipbuilding;

As always, the author extends a special expression of thanks to the dedicated staff at Write Stuff Enterprises, Inc. Proofreader Bonnie Freeman and transcriptionist Mary Aaron worked quickly and efficiently. Indexer Erica Orloff assembled the comprehensive index. Thanks also go to Melody Maysonet, senior editor; Jon VanZile, executive editor; Alex Lieber, former editor; Heather Cohn and Marie Etzler, associate editors; Sandy Cruz, senior art director; Jill Apolinario, Rachelle Donley, Wendy Iverson, Joey Henderson and Dennis Shockley, art directors; Amanda Fowler, assistant to the author; Fred Moll, production manager; David Patten and Tony Wall, executive authors; Marianne Roberts, office manager; Bonnie Bratton, director of marketing; Grace Kurotori, sales and promotions manager; Rafael Santiago, logistics specialist; and Karine Rodengen, project coordinator.

In 1953, Charles Bates Thornton bought a small, California-based microwave tube company from Charles Litton and turned it into the highly successful Litton Industries.

CHAPTER ONE

IN SEARCH OF A DESTINY

"Even in the electronics industry, chock-full of whiz kids, Charles Bates Thornton stands out as a wonder."

— *Time* magazine, 1958[1]

A S THE DUST SETTLED from World War II, the future looked very promising to Charles Bates "Tex" Thornton, a man who, as one writer put it, had "a childhood worthy of Horatio Alger but also with the most modern vision for postwar American management that one could imagine."[2]

Like many men and women whose lives had been interrupted by the global conflict, Thornton realized his true potential during the war. Thornton had an idea that involved a new way of doing business, and though that idea would one day bloom into Litton Industries, he first turned his theory loose on the military, ultimately establishing the first system of "statistical control" the armed forces had ever seen.[3]

Along the way, Thornton learned that a business enterprise could be made to operate rationally on an immense scale and that whoever commanded the numbers was in command. After all, nothing operated on a scale more immense than a world war, and logistics win or lose wars.[4]

According to Thornton's philosophy, success or failure didn't depend on what the product was, but on the management of the product, which in turn meant that the product could be almost anything. At Litton Industries, during the company's boom of the 1950s and 1960s, that was exactly the case as Litton turned out everything from faux diamonds to inertial navigation systems.

Thornton was the forerunner of an emerging class in American business for whom knowledge was less about product and more about systems. If used properly, these systems could govern many different types of companies under the same management umbrella.

The Chance of a Lifetime

For a young man with such grand ideas, the founder of Litton Industries had modest beginnings. Thornton was born on July 22, 1913, in the tiny northwest Texas farm town of Goree. Thornton's father was known as "Tex," and his son was called "Bates." It wasn't until he left Texas that "Bates" Thornton became "Tex" Thornton. Tex's father gained international renown by putting out oil well fires with volatile nitroglycerin, and the son inherited his father's fearless quality, for he was not afraid to tackle any problem head on.

Thornton had a strong work ethic all his life. His early employment involved laboring for 10 cents

As a full colonel in the U.S. Army during World War II, Thornton applied the concept of "statistical control" on a grand scale — a practice he would later carry over to Litton Industries.

an hour on rich Texas farm land. But whether out in the fields as a youngster or behind a desk as a grown man, the day started early.

After graduating from high school, Thornton enrolled as an engineering student at Texas Technological College, later changing his major to business. After a failed Plymouth dealership, which he started at age 19, Thornton decided to try life elsewhere. President Franklin D. Roosevelt's New Deal was going full blast, and Washington, D.C. — with its percolating list of new and expanding alphabet-soup government agencies — looked like a good bet for an ambitious young man.

Thornton discovered that he was not the only young man looking for work in Washington at the height of the Great Depression, but on November 1, 1934, he finally landed a job with the Agricultural Adjustment Administration (AAA).

Over the next few years, Thornton devoted himself to the long climb up the ladder of bureaucracy, finally achieving the august rank of "statistician" in the Housing Authority, then part of the Department of the Interior. In the meantime, he attended George Washington University at night, working on a business degree.

As he climbed the bureaucratic ladder, Thornton discovered that his skills involved more than just compiling numbers. Thornton knew what the numbers meant. He knew how to draw information from seemingly aimless and unconnected statistics, boil them down to the essentials and then explain the statistics so that almost anyone could understand them. He grasped the science and art of statistical analysis before the phrase became popular. He knew how to apply analysis to planning, trend forecasting and problem solving.

One of Thornton's typically trenchant reports came to the attention of Assistant Secretary of War for Air Robert Lovett in March 1941. Lovett, who later became secretary of defense, quickly arranged a meeting. Lovett had been recruited to Washington after writing a critical report on the ability of U.S.

aircraft manufacturers to prepare for the war he knew was coming. He explained to Thornton that he foresaw a huge expansion of the Army Air Corps coupled with a critical need to keep track of what would shortly become the largest air force in the world. As a businessman whose livelihood depended on information, Lovett was appalled by the lack of information he found at the highest levels. He arranged to have Thornton released by the Housing Authority to join him on March 6, 1941, as a second lieutenant, a rank that Thornton already held as a reservist. Tex regarded Lovett as his mentor, later donating a chair at Harvard Business School in Lovett's name.

Statistical Control

Thornton was put in charge of a small group of men who provided support for all staff sections. He found that the staff sections had no coordination in production, training or effort.

Then, on December 7, 1941, more than 360 Japanese planes swooped from the sky, unleashing dive bombs and torpedoes on an unsuspecting U.S. Pacific fleet. By the time the attack was over, more than 2,000 military personnel and 400 civilians were dead. Three of the eight battleships — the backbone of the Navy — were sunk and the other five badly damaged. More than 170 planes were destroyed on the ground.

The Japanese attack on Pearl Harbor made Thornton's efforts urgent. Within three months, he was put in charge of Statistical Control, a designation vague enough to allow him a freer hand than if his duties had been specifically

Thornton's Stat Control found that the B-29 (pictured) would be more efficient and less costly in the war over the Pacific than the more popular B-17. *(Photo courtesy of the National Archives.)*

detailed. After a series of whirlwind promotions, in less than a year Thornton became one of the youngest full colonels in the armed forces, in part because he needed clout to do what he had been assigned to do.

The concept of Statistical Control was not new, but it had never been attempted on the scale that Lovett and Thornton envisioned. They wanted a network of statistical officers assigned to each Air Corps command around the globe. These officers would collect, organize and interpret facts and figures on personnel and equipment, with their reports flowing up to headquarters through a command structure headed by Thornton.

Lovett and Thornton developed a plan to find and train men to become statistical officers. The idea was to select them from among the brightest graduates of the nation's business schools. These graduates would then attend Officer Candidate School, with the cream from every class being sent to Harvard Business School for a special two-month course in the use of statistics. These men would then be sent to work for Thornton.

By war's end, what became known as the Harvard "military academy" would train more than 3,000 officers and specialists to work for Thornton. A few of Thornton's men took another training route. One of them was a young bespectacled Harvard junior instructor named Robert Strange McNamara, who left Harvard for a short military education to make him suitable for Thornton's Stat Control.

The Power of Numbers

What began as a small, close-knit operation in Washington grew to include thousands of men in "control units" spread all over the world. They supplied calculations, estimates and facts to the generals who needed something concrete on which to base the decisions that ran the American war effort.

Stat Control, for example, found that transporting 100,000 tons of supplies and equipment from San Francisco to Australia by air — the military's initial inclination — was not the most efficient method. Forty-four ships and 3,200 sailors could do the job more efficiently than 10,022 airplanes and 120,765 air personnel, assuming that more than 10,000 airplanes and 120,000 air personnel were even available.[5]

Stat Control's recommendations were often controversial. When the war in Europe ended, it was assumed that the workhorse B-17 bombers would be transported from Europe to the Pacific, at least until Stat Control took a hard look at the numbers and reported that it would be much more efficient and cost effective to leave the more numerous B-17s in Europe and use the newer B-29s in the Pacific. Not only would moving the B-17s across the world be more expensive than anyone had thought, but the B-17s lacked the flying range needed in the enormous distances of the Pacific.[6] B-29s could drop 28,000 tons of bombs in 15,000 combat hours, compared to the 90,000 hours B-17s needed to drop the same payload.[7]

In the end, the B-17 bombers that had done so much to win the European war were left parked on European airfields, a decision that shocked many experienced military men, who found themselves outflanked by these young officers and their armament of numbers.

Very quickly, Thornton's men emerged as a confident cadre. These men were at ease making critical decisions based, not on expertise in the field, but on facts, numbers, and their own intelligence and common sense. They were accustomed to running the show and having their conclusions accepted as law. That sense of self-confidence was reinforced when Thornton was awarded the Distinguished Service Medal and the Legion of Merit in recognition of his war efforts.

The Whiz Kids

While the honors bestowed on Thornton were commendable, they did not guarantee an income in peacetime. Like virtually all the young men who served in the war, Thornton and his friends in Stat Control talked endlessly about what they would do after the war ended. Unlike most others,

The Ford Whiz Kids (front row) taken at Ford headquarters in 1946. Front row, left to right: Arjay Miller, Francis "Jack" Reith, George Moore, James Wright, Charles Bates "Tex" Thornton, Wilber Andreson, Charles Bosworth, Ben Mills, J. Edward Lundy and Robert McNamara. (Photo courtesy of the Henry Ford Museum & Greenfield Village Research Center.)

however, they came up with a specific plan. The Stat Control officers knew they had been present at the birth of a powerful new professional discipline. There were great possibilities for use of statistical control systems in peacetime production. Thus, Thornton put together a team with the intention of offering it to a large but struggling corporation. The first version of that team was led by Thornton, who, despite all of his experience, was still only 32.

The team printed a brochure touting themselves and sent it off to several hundred companies, but the response was tepid.[8] Then they heard that Ford Motor Company was in trouble and looking for new blood. Given the disappointing response to Thornton's brochure, Thornton and his group opted for a bolder approach. They sent Ford a telegram, figuring that a letter would get lost in the shuffle and a telephone call would not get past the secretary. The telegram wasn't terribly modest, but it worked. Ford met with Thornton, and a deal was struck.

Ford Motor Company was in even worse shape than Thornton and his group suspected when they reported to work on February 1, 1946. To no one's surprise, the company was losing money. Ford had never conducted an internal audit in its 44-year history, and financial practices were so primitive that its capital earned no interest at all. When the money finally was placed in interest-bearing accounts, it began earning $4.5 million a year.

It didn't help that the eager young men of Thornton's team were bitterly resented in some quarters. Considering that they had no experience whatsoever in the automobile business, they were extremely well paid, an average of $10,000 per man when the average worker in the United States was making about $2,500 a year[9] and the Ford Deluxe "6" coupe cost only $1,088.[10]

In addition, they did not easily fit into the corporate culture. While the 10 men had a variety of broad-ranging interests, those interests were not in the car business. In the jargon of Ford, they weren't "car men." At the same time, many of the Ford executives didn't possess knowledge about anything other than the car business.

Prying into everything and asking questions about anything, they became derisively known as the "Quiz Kids," a name taken from a popular radio show. Later, the name was changed to the "Whiz Kids," a nickname that also began as sarcasm before history turned it into a compliment. (Over the years, four of the "Whiz Kids," Thornton, J. Edward Lundy, Arjay Miller and James Wright, would serve on Litton Industries' board of directors.)

Breaking Up

Despite the current legendary status of the Whiz Kids in American business folklore, the unit didn't stay together very long. Unknown to Thornton, Henry Ford II had begun negotiating to bring in another management team, this one from General Motors, which at the time was thought to have the best management in the country. Leading the team was Ernest R. Breech, a classic lifelong "car man," along with his right-hand man, Lewis D. Crusoe, both of them older than Thornton and much more experienced in the car business.[11]

The arrival of Breech, who immediately became Ford's number two man, was a bitter pill. It moved Thornton further away from the top — both Breech and Crusoe now stood in the way — and put an end to the independence to which he'd grown accustomed. Also, both Crusoe and Breech thought that Thornton needed more production experience, while Thornton believed such an approach meant the same old things would be done in the same old ways.

In May 1948, Thornton left Ford Motor Company. At their last meeting, Breech told Thornton, "You ought to be running your own company."[12] Eventually he would, but not right away. After leaving Ford, Thornton allied himself with another titan of American business, Howard Hughes, a man who was as eccentric as he was wealthy — and he was one of the wealthiest men in the world.

Taking Flight

In 1948, Hughes' holdings included the Hughes Aircraft Company in Culver City, California, a subsidiary of the extremely profitable Hughes Tool Company in Houston, which made oil-drilling tools. The aircraft company's most conspicuous endeavor was the publicly ridiculed *Spruce Goose,* a huge wooden flying airplane begun by Hughes in partnership with Henry J. Kaiser early in World War II. The 200-ton craft had flown only once, for 40 seconds, hardly a terrific return on Hughes' $27 million investment but still a significant engineering achievement.

Thornton agreed to join Hughes Tool as a vice president on May 1, 1948. He was charged with studying Hughes Aircraft and making a recommendation about what to do with it. At the time, Hughes Aircraft was regarded as an insignificant "putterer on the fringes of the aircraft industry" that had lost $750,000 the year before on grosses of $2 million.[13] Noah Dietrich, who had been with Hughes since 1925, considered the subsidiary a wasteful self-indulgence on Hughes' part and made

it clear that he would be happy if Thornton recommended that it be closed.

Instead, Thornton found unexpected possibilities for Hughes Aircraft in the military electronics business. To Dietrich's chagrin, Thornton recommended that Hughes Aircraft concentrate on military electronics, an area that had fallen out of favor with big firms like General Electric and Westinghouse amid the postwar boom. There was a niche to be filled, and Hughes Aircraft was in an ideal position to fill it.

A Few Good Men

Thornton also began to assemble the team that eventually came together at Litton Industries. Among his first hires at Hughes was Harvard lawyer George Fenimore, who later joined Thornton at Litton, eventually becoming a senior vice president. He stayed with Thornton through the ups and downs of the years and decades (except for one stint at TRW): Stat Control, Ford, Hughes and Litton.

In 1949, Thornton hired another old Stat Control hand, Roy Ash, as assistant controller.

Howard Hughes (left) and Harry Cain of the Senate War Investigating Committee in front of Hughes' $27 million *Spruce Goose. (Photo courtesy of the National Archives.)*

Ash was brilliant at interpreting numbers and held the distinction of being the only person to receive a Harvard MBA without a day of undergraduate school.[14]

It was in those years that Thornton also met Glen McDaniel, who was president of the Radio-Television Manufacturers Association. McDaniel helped Thornton start Litton Industries, eventually becoming Litton's senior vice president and chairman of the Executive Committee. It would be McDaniel, an attorney, who would write Litton's original incorporation papers.

In an interview years later, McDaniel described Thornton as "a master brain picker." He remembered Thornton's fascination with the electronics industry, finding out about everything from the top people in the business to emerging patterns and trends.[15] "He thought that electronics was going to bring about a tremendous revolution and that it would control everything that moved from pipe organs in the churches to the most complicated industrial controlled equipment."[16]

Under Thornton's guidance, Hughes Aircraft rose rapidly, especially after the Korean War erupted in 1950. It wasn't long before Hughes had a virtual monopoly on the Air Force's electronic requirements. Deliveries to the military rose from $8.6 million in 1949 to almost $200 million four years later. Hughes was practically the sole source for the greatly expanded requirements for advanced fire-control systems, a feat which was followed by Hughes' successful development of the Falcon air-to-air guided missile and several other successful programs.

All Good Things ...

By the end of the 1940s, Thornton's future looked bright indeed, until Dietrich began meddling with Thornton's authority. Howard Hughes had been difficult from the beginning. While he was not available for important decisions, Hughes meddled in insignificant details, from the color of the paint on the walls to vending machine sales. George Fenimore once received a two-and-one-half-page memo from Hughes detailing the procedures for buying and cleaning seat covers for company cars.[17]

Then Dietrich moved in on the Culver City operation, which he once regarded as so insignificant that he wanted to close it down. Thornton asked for a revolving credit line of $35 million for working capital. Dietrich found the amount excessive and fixed the figure at $25 million, ignoring complaints that it wasn't enough. So Hughes Aircraft was reduced to pressuring the Air Force into larger-than-customary partial payments, an embarrassment at the very least.[18]

The relationship among Hughes, Dietrich and the management of Hughes Aircraft crashed and burned. After a series of ultimatums from the management team — plus a meeting with the Defense Department to explain that there was a very real chance that Hughes Aircraft couldn't meet its obligations — it all fell apart. Dietrich, supported by Hughes, took over personal control of Hughes Aircraft by firing Ash, who was acting controller,

and announced his move to Culver City. Fenimore resigned on September 14, 1953, and Thornton resigned soon thereafter, effective October 1.

The Seeds Are Planted

At age 40, Thornton was out of a job, although he'd been looking ahead for quite some time. A letter to Breech, his old boss at Ford, on April 11, 1953, illustrated how he was already thinking about his next move:

"I am disappointed ... but I am not discouraged.... I believe the full potential of an electronics company cannot be realized either militarily or commercially if it is a division of an airframe company. We sell our products to airframe companies and at least some have already indicated to us that, to protect their own competitive position, they would prefer not to buy these products from an electronics division owned by a competitor...."[19]

Thornton eventually learned that an engineer named Charles V. Litton, who owned a small microwave tube company in San Carlos, California, near San Francisco, wanted to sell. Hughes Aircraft had been buying its magnetron tubes from Litton for years, so Thornton knew the company and the product.

Thornton's philosophy to enter the electronics business was to gather a series of high-quality, highly technical component products with high barriers to entry. Thereafter, he could progress to subsystems and then systems. He knew the "crawl before you walk" principle. He knew the high quality of Charlie Litton's products. He also knew that Charlie's company was a "cash cow." The acquisition of that company would be the first building block of his plan.

It wasn't long before the pieces fell into place, though Thornton's interest in Charlie Litton's company did not appear as though it would turn into something major at first. *Fortune* magazine made a comment in its post-mortem story on the Hughes Aircraft troubles that turned out to be an understatement of epic proportions: Once Thornton left Hughes, the article simply stated, he "formed Electro Dynamics Corporation, which has bought one small company and is negotiating for others."

At age 44, President and Chairman of Litton Industries Charles Bates Thornton had a bright future ahead of him.

CHAPTER TWO

A COMPANY IS BORN

1953–1954

"Litton constantly was searching for the best talent in the fields in which it operated. Acquisitions of brick, mortar and equipment never have taken precedence over the human side, whether these men and women of talent were with other companies which were acquired, other firms, or in the Litton organization...."

— Litton Public Relations department, 1961[1]

AFTER HIS UNSATISFACTORY EXPER-iences at Ford and Hughes, Thornton knew what he wanted next: his own company. Working for others, even two of the giants of American business, had been frustrating and ultimately unsuccessful.

He knew exactly where he could start — at Charles Litton's company near San Francisco. Litton, who didn't particularly enjoy the daily chores of running a corporation, was willing to sell and was being wooed by Sylvania and ITT, among others.

But Thornton and the two Hughes colleagues who agreed to join him in the new venture (Roy L. Ash and former Hughes engineer Hugh W. Jamieson) lacked the resources to meet Litton's asking price of $1 million in cash, not to mention another $500,000 needed for working capital.

It was a typical catch-22. Thornton, Ash and Jamieson needed to have Litton virtually in the bag in order to get money they needed from Wall Street, but they needed the Wall Street money in order to put Litton in the bag.

In Search of Support

Thornton's experience at Hughes Aircraft taught him that advanced electronics represented the future for commerce, industry and the military. Mechanical devices of all kinds were rapidly converting to electronics, and, thanks to the Cold War, the military would demand weapons of increasing electronic complexity.

Thornton wanted to create a company populated by smart men and women doing what they loved to do in an atmosphere that brought out the best in each person. He envisioned the whole operation overseen by himself, with the cool, calculating and logical Ash as his number two and Jamieson as chief engineer.

Thornton's vision was a perfect fit with the Stat Control–Whiz Kid philosophy that a top manager can manage anything because management is what makes a business work. What Thornton had in mind was not an electronics company as much as an "electronics-based" company with tentacles spreading as far as he could make them go, a concept that he claimed "would have been evident to any nine-year-old child willing to think about it."[2] According to Glen McDaniel, Thornton "felt that the way to start a new company was to assemble a group of hard-to-make components where the manufacturing process is very exact and very difficult so that competition is not easy. Once you assembled a group of component companies, you could then proceed to develop subsystems and then systems."[3]

Thornton needed to sell his idea to Wall Street to raise capital. One of his earliest targets included

---

In the company's early days, the magnetron tube, used in air navigation and guidance, was Litton Industries' core product.

Roy Ash was Litton's number two man from 1953 until he took a position with the Nixon administration in 1971.

political powerhouse Joseph P. Kennedy, whose son John F. Kennedy was at that time the junior senator from Massachusetts and who became president seven years later.

The Kennedy relationship, however, never worked out. The elder Kennedy informed Thornton that any company taking his money would have to stay away from government contracts because he wanted his son John to run for president one day, and it would not do for the family to be involved with a firm that made "weapons of war."[4] But government contracts, especially defense contracts, were a vital component in Thornton's vision of the future. Kennedy's second point was even more unpalatable. If Kennedy put up the money, he wanted control of the company. After his experience

with Ford and Hughes, Thornton didn't intend to hand control over to someone else.[5]

As Thornton and Ash made the Wall Street rounds, their insistence on control began to look like a deal killer. "No one wanted to give us 60 or 70 percent of the company," Ash explained later. "We fought for it on the theory that we were delivering more than just management. We were delivering a particular kind of management that had proven it could achieve incredible numbers."[6]

They finally found an interest at Lehman Brothers, the prestigious Wall Street investment house. Lehman Brothers listened because Thornton and a Lehman Brothers partner, Joe Thomas, had earlier put together a package to try to buy Hughes Aircraft, an offer that was at first encouraged, but then rejected, by the mercurial Howard Hughes. Thomas, a grandson of the firm's founder, Robert Lehman, was a man whose opinion was respected.

In a 1963 *Time* magazine cover story, Thornton recalled how "I told 'em that I wanted to start a company that would become a strong blue chip in the scientific and technological environment of the future. It would be a balanced company, not just engineering, not just manufacturing, not just financial. You can't win a ball game with only a pitcher and a catcher, and you can't have a strong company unless it's balanced."[7]

Most of those who heard the pitch were impressed, but not everyone was a believer, especially after Thornton's boast that he would achieve $100 million in sales within five years. One Lehman partner, Paul Mazur, argued that Thornton displayed more braggadocio than brains and that any Lehman investment in this windy Texan would shortly be swirling down the drain. Years later, when Litton Industries was the fastest-growing corporation in American business history, Mazur readily admitted, "I was wrong. Thornton delivered far better than he talked."[8]

Fortunately for Thornton, Ash and Jamieson, Mazur's skepticism wasn't shared by others, although it took some time for Lehman to put the unique package together. In the meantime, Thornton enlisted the help of McDaniel to assist in the negotiations and to help draft the paperwork for the new company's charter and bylaws.[9]

They called the company "Electro Dynamics," a cumbersome name that Thornton liked because anyone who heard it would know that it was involved in technology. As it turned out, the name was so temporary that it was virtually irrelevant. For a $1,000 fee, Electro Dynamics was incorporated in the state of Delaware on October 2, 1953, essentially just a shell company waiting for the details to coalesce so that it could buy Litton Industries and really get moving.

Fancy Footwork

By this point, timing had become a problem. The option to buy Litton's company was edging closer to expiration, which Lehman Brothers knew all too well. The closer it came to the deadline, the more concessions the savvy investors hoped to get

Glen McDaniel, Litton's first general counsel, drafted the Electro Dynamics incorporation papers and helped Thornton negotiate with Lehman Brothers, a renowned Wall Street investment firm.

out of Thornton in order to gain a larger share of the company, perhaps even overall control. As a result, it was increasingly difficult to get any action at all out of Lehman Brothers.

Charles Litton was skittish, too. Other, more sizable entities that didn't have to go looking for money were interested in his company, and Litton was growing impatient. Thornton, who had been on a killer schedule bouncing back and forth between California and New York City, met with Litton and turned his considerable powers of persuasion on the restless engineer. He not only convinced Litton to wait, but also talked him into a new deal. Settling for $300,000 up front, Litton agreed to accept the rest of the money in installments, if necessary.[10]

Thornton, however, didn't have $300,000. To get it, he went to Ransom Cook, president of the American Trust Company in San Francisco, which was Litton's bank. Cook agreed to loan Thornton $300,000 based on the cash flow of Litton's company, with which he was quite familiar. Cook's rescue put Thornton in a position to exercise his option on Litton, with or without Lehman Brothers.

After Thornton returned to New York City, the deal with Lehman Brothers came to a speedy conclusion. Although such deals would become common many years later, it was an extraordinary move for its time. Using somebody else's money, Thornton, Ash and Jamieson got what they wanted — complete control.

When Lehman Brothers agreed to back Thornton and his grandiose plan for a "major electronics company," the firm created a unique financial package to make the deal work. To raise the $1.5 million needed to buy Charles Litton's company, Thornton and Lehman partner Joe Thomas divided the sum into 52 units of $29,200 each: 20 bonds worth $1,200 each to equal $24,000; 50 shares of 5 percent preferred stock to equal $5,000; and 2,000 shares par 10 cents to equal $200.

Each bond was subsequently converted into common stock at $10.75 per share, with the preferred shares converted into common at $1 per share. With subsequent stock dividends and splits, within 10 years each $29,200 unit was worth $3.2 million.

The deal was signed on November 26, 1953, but it wasn't until December 3 that all 52 of the "units" or "packages" were sold to generate

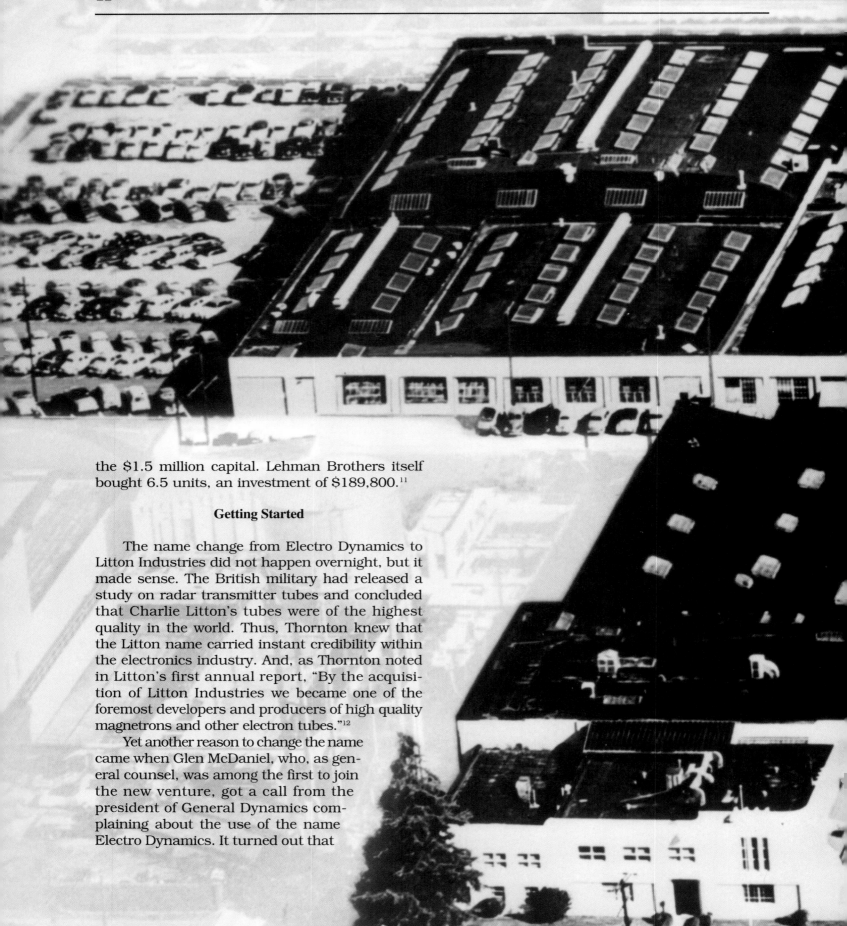

the $1.5 million capital. Lehman Brothers itself bought 6.5 units, an investment of $189,800.[11]

Getting Started

The name change from Electro Dynamics to Litton Industries did not happen overnight, but it made sense. The British military had released a study on radar transmitter tubes and concluded that Charlie Litton's tubes were of the highest quality in the world. Thus, Thornton knew that the Litton name carried instant credibility within the electronics industry. And, as Thornton noted in Litton's first annual report, "By the acquisition of Litton Industries we became one of the foremost developers and producers of high quality magnetrons and other electron tubes."[12]

Yet another reason to change the name came when Glen McDaniel, who, as general counsel, was among the first to join the new venture, got a call from the president of General Dynamics complaining about the use of the name Electro Dynamics. It turned out that

An aerial view of Litton's first general offices and main research and manufacturing plant, the Electronic Equipments division, in Beverly Hills, California.

General Dynamics had a small, obscure division with the same name in New Jersey.[13] Officially the name change didn't occur until August 16, 1954. Charles Litton was paid a small fee for the use of his name.

Thus Thornton's company became Litton Industries, with Thornton as the new company's president and chairman of the board, Ash as secretary-treasurer and Jamieson as executive staff engineer.

The first order of business was to set up a new headquarters. Electro Dynamics had been working out of a rented garage in West Los Angeles. Clearly, such a location was not sufficient or suitably prestigious. In April 1954, Litton made its headquarters in a 165,000-square-foot former sewing machine factory in Beverly Hills.

As he did in Stat Control and again at Ford, Thornton began assembling his team. The new company had two groups of management, one in Beverly Hills, the other in San Carlos. Some of the titles were so vague they could mean almost anything, but the company was similar to a professional sports team, which drafts the best

THE MAN BEHIND THE NAME

History has not been kind to Charles V. Litton, who, thanks to the deal he made to sell Litton Industries in 1953, has been characterized as a "gold-plated loser,"[1] to use one of the more charitable descriptions. Yet Litton's world-class magnetron power tubes were rated by the British government as "the best"[2] — an enviable distinction that underscores the man's brilliance.

On paper, the deal Thornton struck to buy Litton's company does look like a poor one. Litton took a cash price of $1.05 million ($816,414 for stock and $233,586 for patents).[3] He also accepted a small fee as a consultant, paid out over several years.

Charlie Litton's refusal to accept stock, which would have made him fabulously wealthy, has been the object of scorn ever since the company was sold. The same 1966 magazine article that had so harshly characterized him also calculated that if Litton had taken stock instead of cash, he would have been worth $150 million 13 years later.[4] Yet, considering that Litton had lived through the Great Depression, his lack of faith in stock is not surprising.

Charles Litton still got exactly what he wanted. With 250 employees and annual sales of $3 million, his company was a highly respected maker of magnetron tubes — microwave radiation–emitting tubes that helped guide the missiles of American fighter jets to their targets. His product was better than the product of his larger competitors (Sylvania, for example, which also wanted to buy Litton's company, ITT, G.E., and Raytheon), thanks to superior quality control.

Litton was no empire builder. In spirit, he was much closer to Thomas Edison than to Henry Ford, or to Charles Bates Thornton, for that matter. Tall (6 feet 3 inches) and slender, he was a fiddler and a tinkerer, a man of varied interests who started Litton Industries in a San Carlos garage, near San Francisco. He owned and flew his own helicopter and airplane and was a competent machinist, electronics engineer and glass blower. He was a radio ham operator and a music lover who built his own stereo and radio equipment.

In an interview several years after the sale, Litton explained that an estate consultant had informed him that his company, essentially a proprietorship, would probably die when he did, thanks in large part to the robust inheritance tax laws of the time.[5]

Decades before the phrase became popular, quality of life was important to Litton. His company had grown too big for his comfort, and he wanted to move to Grass Valley, a small town in the California foothills not far from Lake Tahoe, to start another company.

With Thornton's assurances that Litton's "people" would be taken care of — as would his name, which would remain on the company — Litton made the deal and moved Litton Engineering to his new facility in Grass Valley.

"I had a special situation and I knew … that a million dollars would carry out my plan," he said. "All I wanted … was enough money … so that I could continue to live the way I wanted and keep busy. It's worked out fine. I need a hundred million dollars like I need three thumbs."[6]

Charles V. Litton died at age 69 in Carson City, Nevada, on November 16, 1972. Before Thornton purchased his business, he had led the market in magnetron tubes, and today, that original business upon which Litton Industries was founded — the business that became known as the Electron Tube Division and was later renamed the Electron Devices Division (EDD) — continues to lead the field in state-of-the-art vacuum electron devices.

all-around athlete available, then figures out how to use that athlete.

In one of the most important hires in Litton history, Dr. Henry Singleton, a brilliant former MIT professor and Naval Academy graduate whom Thornton had met at Hughes, was lured away from a position at North American Aviation to run navigation and flight control. Singleton would later be responsible for jump-starting Litton's enormous long-term success in inertial navigation.

In addition to McDaniel and Singleton, the "draftees" included George Kozmetsky, who had been in the same class at Harvard Business School as Ash, to run "computers and controls." Harry Gray, a former Greyhound executive, was put in charge of "commercial program planning." Myles L. Mace, a Harvard colleague of Robert McNamara who was both an attorney and a business Ph.D., ran the Electronic Equipments division.

By the end of its first year in business, Litton Industries had already acquired several companies: three Colorado-based firms, manufacturers of precision resistors; the Birklan Corporation in Mount Vernon, New York, which produced potentiometers; Digital Control Systems, Inc., in La Jolla, California, where Litton set up its research and development lab for electronic computers and controls; West Coast Electronics in Los Angeles; and USECO, Inc., in Glendale, California, manufacturer of standard electronics hardware.[14]

Litton Industries' first annual report came out in 1954. The 16-page publication was modest by

Left: Harry J. Gray, among the first Litton executives recruited, became general manager of the Components division.

Center: Dr. Henry Singleton was the mastermind behind one of Litton's signature products, the inertial navigation system. His work spawned one of Litton's largest divisions, Guidance and Control.

Right: Dr. Myles L. Mace, also among the first Litton executives recruited, became a corporate vice president and general manager of the Electronic Equipments division.

later standards, when Litton annual reports became famous for their size and grand style, but Thornton used the report to express the company's mission and high hopes for the future:

"The name of Litton Industries is significant in the electronics industry — an industry which I believe has almost unlimited growth potential. Your company is making good progress toward its objective of becoming one of the major companies in the industry. Its success can be as great as the abilities and talents of its personnel and the interest and cooperation of its investors."[15]

Or, as *Time* magazine said several years later, "… a corporation that is dedicated to the relentless pursuit of the future."[16]

Charles Thornton (top) and Roy Ash at a Litton Industries annual stockholder session (circa late 1950s).

CHAPTER THREE

INTERLOCKING PIECES

1954–1959

"All industries have gone through a maturing phase, and a few companies emerge to stabilize the industry. In five years or so, a few dominant companies will emerge from electronics. Litton is going to be one of them."

— Charles Bates "Tex" Thornton, 1958[1]

TEX THORNTON HAD ALWAYS claimed that it wouldn't have mattered if Charles Litton had refused to sell his company because Thornton had his eye on several others. If it had not been Litton, it would have been something else. "Litton was just one of a number of companies that we already had lined up," Thornton told *Forbes* magazine. "When we started, we hit the track running hard."[2]

With its management team solidly in place, Litton Industries began to grow in a way that no other corporation in American business history had ever grown, fueled by long hours, hard work and opportunistic fervor. Vacations for Litton's management came rarely, if ever. Thornton's inner circle were given fair warning: "You think you know what work is? You think you know all about long hours and putting out a maximum effort? Well, you haven't seen anything yet. Forget it. We're going to get in shape. We're going to fight a war in peacetime."[3]

Charles Litton's old company was the perfect base from which to take advantage of the huge increase in military spending brought on by the Cold War. In each year of the Eisenhower presidency (1952 to 1960), more than half the national budget went toward defense. Such spending was spurred by the widespread fear of communism. The Korean War, the growing American involvement in Vietnam

and the Suez crisis in the Middle East — combined with Secretary of State John Foster Dulles' strategy of nuclear brinkmanship — all pushed the government to increase its military spending.[4]

When the Soviet Union launched the *Sputnik* satellite in 1957, visions of Soviet nuclear bombs hurtling from the heavens panicked Americans, despite the fact that the United States maintained a clear military advantage in conventional and nuclear weapons. For without a sophisticated guidance system, *Sputnik* was little more than an unguided piece of metal. Soviet Premier Nikita Khrushchev admitted that, "Our missiles were still imperfect in performance and insignificant in number. Taken by themselves, they didn't represent much of a threat to the United States."[5] But perception rather than reality often decided victories and defeats in the Cold War. The race for space was on, and a nimble company such as Litton was perfectly positioned to take advantage of such a race. In his letter to shareholders, Thornton described Litton's role and mission:

Litton had a knack for seeing what would be useful in the not-too-distant future. The Litton-20, for example, was a digital desktop computer "capable of doing mathematical calculations of 50 men working for one year with standard desk calculators."

"Today our national attention is directed to the technological competition between the two great powers of the world. Events in outer space arrest the interest of all walks of life. Prosperity, the absence of a shooting war, and a life of abundance are taken for granted.

"But behind this apparent well-being stand those elements of American industry dedicated to creating and producing ever more meaningful products to strengthen and serve industry, commerce, and our national defense. It is to this end that the people of Litton Industries have dedicated their talents and energies during the past fiscal year."[6]

The Sum of Parts

For a relatively small corporation, Litton embarked on an unparalleled buying spree, purchasing a number of little-known companies that made printed circuits, computers, and communications and navigation equipment. In its first three years Litton completed 13 acquisitions.[7]

This early acquisitiveness was particularly impressive considering that aside from his house,

Thornton's net worth was only about $30,000 when he bought Litton Industries using borrowed money.[8] According to the 1955 annual report, acquisitions boosted sales 300 percent over the previous year. One year later, Litton proudly declared that "our employment was up almost 40 percent from last year."

But it wasn't just growth for growth's sake. "We have never acquired companies as such," Thornton said. "We have bought time, a market, a product line, a plant, a research team, a sales force. It would take us years to duplicate all this from scratch."[9]

Historically, most American corporations remained devoted to their core business. Ford and General Motors made cars, for instance, while oil companies concentrated on how to get the viscous fluid out of the ground and to consumers. The relationships among the various parts of these companies were clear, and the links were obvious; all of the parts pointed at one final all-important product, and the men defined themselves as "car men" or "oil men."

Litton was creating a new way to do business. With electronics becoming a part of every aspect of modern life, an "electronics-based" business had a broad definition.

Arguably the first conglomerate, Litton rapidly turned a small business into something much bigger, with all of the various parts integrated into a greater whole. "Two plus two equals five," explained George Fenimore, who had also worked with Thornton at Ford and Hughes. "The magic word that Tex and Roy Ash started using was 'synergy.'"[10]

Another Litton innovation was its way of sensing a new market, then finding the right strategy to sell to that market. Its engineers didn't build a better mouse trap and wait for customers. Instead, it saw that better electronic mouse traps would be needed in the not-too-distant future and figured out how to acquire the component companies necessary to make, market and sell them. In short, first Litton spotted the market. Then it found a way to make the product or bought several different companies that, when put together, could make the product.

Charles Thornton (seated), along with Roy Ash (standing), grew a young Litton Industries into a major "electronics-based" company.

Above: General Counsel Glen McDaniel (second from left), President and CEO Charles Thornton (second from right) and Vice President Roy Ash (far right) celebrate Litton Industries' first listing on the New York Stock Exchange in 1957.

Right: Thornton (center) celebrates Litton's first million in profits on January 24, 1956.

Litton's strategy proved successful. By the end of fiscal 1956, its profits had exceeded $1 million, and the executives had a party to celebrate the event.[11] On July 30, 1957, its stock was listed on the New York Stock Exchange, making Litton Industries one of the youngest companies to make the Big Board. (Litton had been on the American Exchange since September 26, 1956.)[12]

The Man Behind the Curtain

By the late 1950s, the press began to notice Litton, showering the company and its management team with plaudits. In 1958, *Fortune* magazine published an article titled "Litton Shoots for the Moon." *Time* followed with its own favorable coverage later that year. Litton, declared *Time*, was "a wonder."[13] And *Forbes* wrote that Thornton "was a gifted manager of men and money" who "displayed the talents of a prophet, bird dog, and T-formation quarterback."[14] Not to be outdone, *Time* said that he resembled "a tough trail boss in a TV western."[15] Rhapsodizing about the team of Ash and Thornton, *Fortune* described them as "logical Roy and intuitive Tex."[16]

In the many bouquets tossed to Thornton, there were times when the journalists didn't seem to be writing about the same man. He was described as persuasive and articulate, but it was also said that his speech couldn't keep up with the speed of his thoughts, rendering him almost inarticulate at times. He was deliberate and he was intuitive, all at once. He hated time off, or what he called "useless leisure," but he loved to escape to his Southern California ranch, saddle up and ride out into the countryside to get away from it all and think things over. He made decisions quickly; he took his time.

Research and Development

In addition to acquiring new companies, Litton also looked inward, concentrating on research and development in a few key areas, paid for with profits plowed back into the company. Under Harry Gray, Litton's original microwave tube business formed the core of what became the Electron Tube Division. During the 1950s, the division developed cooker magnetrons and a microwave oven and expanded into other crossed-field devices such as

the M-carcinotron for the B-52 ECM system. The division also expanded its product line to include high-power klystrons. The L-303 klystron became a pacesetter for airport radar that is still being manufactured today.[17]

George Kozmetsky ran the research and development work in defense computers, which not only spawned Litton's future command and control (C²) business but provided a technology base for other Litton avionics computer products as well.[18] Dr. Henry Singleton's team of scientists and engineers worked on an inertial guidance device for airborne navigation systems, which eventually became Litton Industries' signature product.

The technologies developed by Kozmetsky and Singleton spawned Litton's first two internally grown, and soon-to-be-largest, divisions. Out of that early R&D crucible sprang both the Guidance and Control and the Data Systems divisions.

Guidance and Control was launched to exploit the market for airborne navigation with systems based on Singleton's work. Data Systems had a similar mission in applying Litton's advanced computer technology to the automation of military operations in the harsh tactical ground and airborne environments.[19]

Kozmetsky's work led to the emergence of Litton Industries as the pioneering developer of information technology–based systems. Singleton's work led to a signature Litton Industries navigation product destined to be found on every major ship, missile, spacecraft and aircraft.[20]

While the theory of inertial navigation had been well known for many years, modern inertial navigation really began in 1950 when the Department of Defense requested a practical, self-contained navigation system that needed no external stimuli or data to function. As explained in Litton's 1956 annual report, "Dead reckoning, celestial navigation, radio and radar-controlled flight — all of the commonly used techniques for the navigation and guidance of missiles and aircraft — have major shortcomings in military operations."[21]

In 1957, Norman H. Moore was vice president and general manager of Litton's Electron Tube Division, which developed cooker magnetrons and a microwave oven.

By 1953, the first-generation inertial navigation systems had been developed at MIT and were being used in test flights. One of the problems of these early prototypes was that each system weighed some 2,800 pounds, which was much too heavy for practical application.

In its most elementary form, an inertial navigation system is an apparatus that tells pilots where they are at any instant in time and how to steer the aircraft (automatically or manually) to get to where they want to go. The most important components are three gyroscopes that provide information on roll, pitch and yaw; three accelerometers that sense changes in velocity along three axes; and a computer that integrates the information into position, speed, attitude, distance and time to destination.

The system computes how far away and in what direction the craft is from its starting point and destination by measuring and "remembering" acceleration second by second. No matter how many turns, speed changes, climbs or dives the plane makes, the system continuously gives the pilot the location as well as the ground speed and attitude of the aircraft. Drift angle and range wind information are also provided for bombing and missile-firing purposes. The gyros maintain a fixed reference in space and, in conjunction with a computer, also make corrections for the turning of the earth, wind and, in the case of ships, waves.

Today's inertial navigation systems can be miniaturized into a package smaller than a basketball and weighing less than 20 pounds, although they come in many different shapes, sizes, capabilities and uses. Modern systems may contain their own computers or rely on a master computer in the aircraft that also performs other tasks. Launch vehicles, missiles and spacecraft use variations on this theme.

Aircraft navigating by inertial guidance cannot be pinpointed by an enemy, unlike those navigating by other guidance systems, such as radar. Because an inertial system does not depend on outside sources for information, there is no signal for an enemy to track. In the early and mid-1950s, a lightweight inertial guidance system was something that military aircraft desperately needed.

It was a boon for Litton when Singleton joined the company because he was one of the most

One of the first men to join Litton, Dr. Henry E. Singleton holds an early version of Litton's inertial navigation system, one of Litton's key products that he is largely responsible for masterminding.

experienced men in the country in the field of inertial navigation. He had already been involved in similar research at North American Aviation.

Singleton's team had to meet three simple but extremely difficult requirements: An inertial guidance system had to be free of any need for inflight data from the ground, it had to be small, and it had to be light. The task was so complex that many doubted whether it could be achieved at all.

Undaunted, Litton built a state-of-the-art laboratory and preliminary production facilities by the end of 1956, as described in that year's annual report: "One can appreciate the minuteness of this work when it is realized that certain of the components of inertial guidance systems are connected by wires 1/20th the diameter of a human hair."[22]

After several million dollars had gone into Litton's inertial guidance program, Litton won a $1 million Department of Defense development contract to make Singleton's system operational within a year. The contract gave Litton a window of opportunity that no one else had, and Singleton's team met the deadline. When the system became operational in 1958, it put Litton years ahead of its rivals.[23]

The hard work paid off. By the end of fiscal 1959, Litton's inertial equipment had been installed in the Navy's Grumman Hawkeye E-2C, an early warning aircraft. Litton also had contracts to make guidance systems for the Grumman A-6 Intruder (a carrier-based, all-weather attack aircraft) and Lockheed's P-3 Orion (an anti-submarine patrol aircraft).

On the international front, West Germany's air force selected Litton's LN-3 inertial guidance system for the Lockheed F-104G Starfighter, which set a trend for similar procurements by Canada, Italy, Belgium and Holland.[24]

It was this program that launched Litton into the high-volume inertial navigation business well ahead of the rest of the world. Litton, in fact, started two new divisions — LITEF, based in Freiburg, Germany, and Litton Italia, based in Rome, Italy — to license produce the LN-3 inertial navigation system for the F-104 Starfighter. Over the 35-year life span of the LN-3 program, LITEF had over $200 million in LN-3 sales, which was far more than any other Litton division, and Litton Italia had over $130 million.[25]

Typical of the Litton strategy, its inertial guidance system was first developed for military purposes and later sold to civilian airlines and aircraft all over the world. Litton was the first company to have a commercially certified inertial navigation system for airliners.[26] American Airlines was its first domestic customer, and when Air France equipped its Boeing 707 in October 1967, it became Litton's first international customer.[27] On August 26, 1983, Air France received Litton's 20,000th inertial navigation system. So strong was Litton in this field that at one point in the 1960s it had 90 percent of the inertial navigation market.[28] The 1961 selling price of these systems was upward of $150,000 each.[29]

While work on the navigation side of the young company was proceeding in its Guidance and Control laboratory, down the hall in the Data Systems lab, scientists and engineers were building a strange-looking computer. Its memory resembled a quarter slice of an oil drum spinning on an axis like an old Edison gramophone recording. Although a far cry from today's multimegabyte semiconductor memories, the magnetic recording technology it used to store data was similar to what can be found

Once considered "classified" by the Navy, the Litton Airborne Digital Computer, or "flying brain," combined navigation, flight control, weapon firing and fuel management in one computer. Shown below are the logic board (on right) and the commutator and drum for the T2V-1 Interim Central Control Computer.

in the hard disk drives of the modern-day PC. Those pioneering information technologists had an idea that by combining their "drum memory" with specially designed digital circuits, they could produce a computing machine capable of processing data in "real time." A real-time capability meant that information in a rapidly changing environment could be collected and digested fast enough for someone to react to the changes as they were occurring — an ideal capability to bring to the battlefield, where friendly and enemy movements in the air and on the ground are many and frequent.[30]

Quick to recognize an opportunity, the entrepreneurs at Litton seized upon the idea and obtained a contract from the Navy to develop the first Airborne Tactical Data System (ATDS) in 1958. Designed to fly aboard a Super-Constellation aircraft, the job of the ATDS was to automate many of the tedious tasks associated with surveillance and control of a given airspace. Although Litton sold only one system to the Navy, it was the precursor to the next generation of airborne and ground-based tactical data systems that proved to be a wildly successful business for the company, generating several billion dollars of revenue to date. Following ATDS, an aircraft carrier-based version (CB/STDS) was designed for the Navy's Grumman-built E-2 early warning and control aircraft. Improvements in capacity and

performance, made possible by brilliant use of new semiconductor technology, resulted in a system that has been a mainstay in Navy command and control to the present day.[31]

Sensing a similar need in the tactical ground environment, Litton succeeded in winning a contract with the Marine Corps for a prototype Marine Tactical Data System (MTDS). Designed to operate in and survive the rigors of a Marine amphibious assault operation, the system automated air surveillance and weapons control operations in that fast-changing environment. A production contract for the AN/TYQ-2 Tactical Air Operations Center followed in 1962, after a highly successful field test of the prototype.[32]

Those sentinel programs provided a solid foundation for the launch of Litton Data Systems as a separate operating division. In the following 35-plus years, Data Systems extended Litton's reach and reputation as a premier supplier of information technology solutions to a wide range of military command and control needs across all the military services.[33]

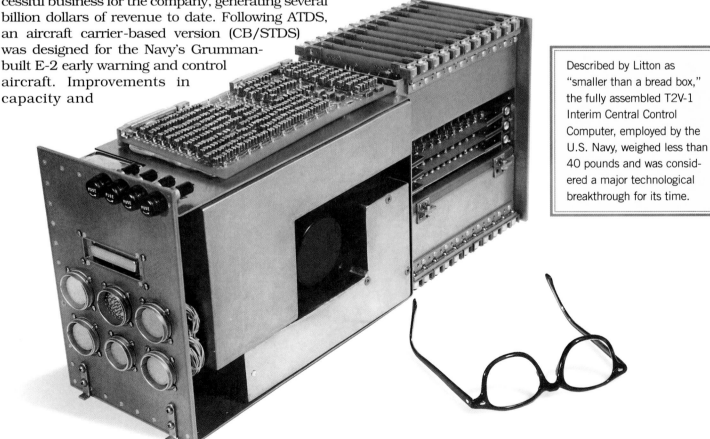

Described by Litton as "smaller than a bread box," the fully assembled T2V-1 Interim Central Control Computer, employed by the U.S. Navy, weighed less than 40 pounds and was considered a major technological breakthrough for its time.

A Calculated Decision

In what McDaniel called "our first non-electronic"[34] — and first truly large — acquisition, Litton Industries bought the Monroe Calculating Machine Company in 1957 through exchange of stock and cash worth $18 million.[35] With sales of over $40 million the year it was acquired, the Monroe Calculating Machine Company, a respected manufacturer of calculating and adding machines, brought to Litton a strong position in the field of business and office machines, including 325 sales and service branches.[36]

Founded in 1912, Monroe had not kept pace with technology, and its all-mechanical components were in serious danger of being left behind in the electronic age. Monroe's situation was similar to Charles Litton's in the early 1950s. It was a privately held company with no public stock,

The Monroe Calculating Machine Company was acquired by Litton in 1957 and was Litton's largest acquisition at the time. A manufacturer of calculating and adding machines, Monroe paved the way for Litton's move into commercial markets.
Facing Page: Litton added technology to the all-mechanical components of Monroe's and Svenska's products. The Monroe/Svenska cash register, for example, featured new "power penny keys" to increase speed and accuracy.

and the Monroe family had an estate problem — inheritance taxes would probably kill the company and leave the heirs with little or nothing. Even if they managed to keep the company, upgrading the mechanical components to electronics would have been prohibitively expensive. As a result, the family wanted to sell.

Thornton used the same sales pitch that had worked with Charles Litton years earlier, though

on a much larger scale. While Monroe did what it did better than anyone, times were changing. The addition of Litton's electronic know-how to the respected Monroe name and mechanism would guarantee that Monroe would continue to be respected and successful for many years to come, instead of merely drifting into sad obsolescence.

In exchange, the deal gave Litton the extensive sales and service outlets of Monroe, and it saved Litton a great deal of time in penetrating commercial markets. For Litton, it was a quantum leap. As McDaniel said, "… He [Thornton] wanted, through military contracts, to develop a computer that you could put in a coffee can, and then that could be the basis of a whole series of office machines."[37] Fred Sullivan, Monroe's president at the time of the acquisition and one of the architects of the deal, joined Litton to run the Monroe division.

In return for Litton stock worth about $17 million in market value, but only $1.4 million in book value, Litton acquired a company whose conservatively estimated net worth was about $16 million, one that was earning about $2 million a year and one that was twice as large as Litton itself.[38] It was a classic Litton maneuver: buy a troubled business that had a high-profile name in a specific field.

The Monroe acquisition also was important for another reason — diversity. It helped wean Litton away from excess dependence on government contracts. Without Monroe, 70 percent of Litton's business was government related. With Monroe, that figure fell to 50 percent.[39]

In an in-house memo dated March 13, 1958, Standard & Poor's reviewed Litton Industries after extensive research and interviews. The then-confidential memo provides a good snapshot of Litton at that time.

"These people tell a very confident story. They think that they are going places and are not reluctant to say so. Up to now, we certainly cannot fault them on the record.... They plan to break into the smaller type digital computer field through Monroe, which has the marketing organization they needed. They admit this field is rough, but think they can carve out a position in it...."[40]

Impressive as it was, the Monroe acquisition confused a lot of people. As Thornton later explained, "We got calls from people saying, 'We thought you were in the electronics business. What are you doing with an office machine company?' You wanted to say, 'What the hell do you

Litton applied its technological know-how to the Litton-20 to make digital computers for the commercial market smaller and less expensive.

think electronics is? We don't sell electrons, we sell products.'"[41]

The Quest for Synergy

Growing as fast as it was, Litton needed more space and bought 63 acres in the San Fernando Valley at Woodland Hills. Reportedly unhappy about the frenzied pace of growth through acquisition, Jamieson left in 1958 to start his own electronics components company. Mace departed not long afterward. Singleton left in 1960 to start his own hugely successful company, Teledyne, Inc.

Meanwhile, Litton's buying spree continued. In 1958, new acquisitions included Airtron, Inc., which manufactured specialized microwave components and equipment for radar and other microwave communication.[42] That same year, Litton acquired the Westrex Corporation, a subsidiary of the Western Electric Company. Westrex's primary business was in sound equipment for the motion picture industry for Hollywood movie studios and theaters all over the world. McDaniel noted that Westrex's 36 foreign offices serving 50 foreign countries "took us abroad and gave us an international presence" for the first time.[43]

That international presence helped set the stage for Litton's 1960 acquisition of Svenska Dataregister, a Swedish company that already had a foothold in the American cash register market, the first challenge to National Cash Register in a half-century.

This, too, was an increasingly common strategy. "We always liked to get into a field that had been a monopoly," McDaniel said. "The monopoly always made enemies, and people are pleased to have a choice."[44]

The acquisition looked promising as part of Litton's strategy for synergy among its operations, and it would also give Litton a stronger presence in Europe. Combine Svenska's cash registers with Monroe's calculators and adding machines — which had already been boosted by Litton electron-

ics — and Litton was ready to make a big move on the "point of sale" industry.[45]

Unfortunately, it soon became cheaper to make cash registers in the United States. Thanks to the superior network of American suppliers, Sweden could not possibly make a cash register that could compete with one made in the United States.[46] Svenska was sold to the Svenska Swedish management in 1968.

Commercial Developments

By the end of 1959, Litton had acquired 27 companies in six years and had made a number of developments in the commercial market. That year, over half of the company's sales were directed at the commercial-industrial market rather than the military.[47]

The leap toward commercial business was largely due to the Monroe acquisition. Litton now offered a broad line of business machines, including a printing multiplier and several models of adding machines and accounting machines. In addition, the Monroe division introduced the Monrobot, an electronic billing machine that rented for only $700 a month, compared to the IBM 7070's $24,000-per-month price tag.[48]

Other commercial developments included the introduction in 1956 of the Litton-20, a digital (rather than analog) computer for solving differential equations. The techniques used in developing the Litton-20 also led to military contracts to assemble computers that could solve more complex problems with less complex equipment.[49]

Litton Industries had come a long way in only a few years. The company's 1959 annual report declared that net sales were over $125 million, thanks to its "closely integrated, logically related operating divisions," whose major fields of endeavor were business machines, communications equipment, precision components, and military equipment and systems.[50]

But as fast as Litton had grown in the 1950s, that growth would seem slow indeed compared to what was about to happen.

In 1964, Litton moved its corporate headquarters to this stately building on Santa Monica Boulevard in Beverly Hills.

CHAPTER FOUR

A TECHNOLOGICAL CASCADE

1960–1967

"For it is the vigor of this nation's industrial base that will determine our posture as the leader of the free world. We must fortify our own strength if we are to show the way for free men to follow. Such is our responsibility and duty today."

— Charles Thornton and Roy Ash, 1961[1]

THE EARLY TO MID-1960s was a golden time for Litton Industries, an era of growth, expansion, praise and success rarely equaled in American business history. Litton was the fastest growing company on the New York Stock Exchange, and its common stock was highly valued. (In 1961, for instance, one share of common stock sold for $140.)[2] In 1960, the company employed more than 17,400, with annual sales exceeding $200 million.[3] Three years later it boasted 43,000 employees and had become the nation's 100th largest corporation.[4] By 1965, Litton's sales had increased by more than 30,000 percent since its first year,[5] and by 1966, it had 146 plants in 21 states and 12 foreign countries.[6]

This supernova of a conglomerate, which had modest beginnings only a few years earlier, now was envied all across the business landscape for its vision, aggressiveness and original thinking.

Fame and Fortune

The press eagerly chronicled Litton's success and freewheeling style in story after story, with *Time* magazine describing it in 1963 as "an amorphous giant with interests and appetites as broad as the universe."[7] The typical coverage used words that were new to business language, words like "synergy" and "niche marketing," words that the journalists picked up from the Litton executives themselves. Other phrases were unique to Litton's culture and were mostly used in-house. For example, "technological cascade" was what Litton executives called their method of finding a new way to capitalize on a field that they had recently entered.[8]

"In the sixties, Litton was magic and everyone felt it," recalled Fred O'Green, who left Lockheed to join Litton in 1962 and who would go on to become Litton's president in 1972. "We were growing by leaps and bounds. It was a free-flowing environment. You could walk down the production line and talk to workers who had degrees in philosophy and everything else. It was a very enlightened group of people. They were attracted because of the magic of Litton."[9]

At Harvard Business School—the same school where Thornton sent candidates for his Stat Control group during World War II — Litton was studied as the archetype of the high-flying con-

For many years, the Litton name was most closely associated with microwave ovens, which the company began producing in 1965.

glomerate of a high-flying time. Ash and Thornton repeatedly protested that the word "conglomerate" implied "a mess." They suggested "multi-industry company" as an alternative, a suggestion to which no one else paid the slightest attention.

What few problems existed were visible only in retrospect. Ironically, many of them were a direct result of Litton's stunning rise.

"You could say that there was quite a self-assured air at Litton then," said George Fenimore, who joined Litton in 1965 to run its public relations department and retired 21 years later as senior vice president and corporate secretary. "They believed that they could do almost anything and manage everything."[10]

Fenimore recalled that at one point in the mid-1960s, although it already had close to 400 foreign and domestic companies, Litton still was buying what seemed like a company a week.[11] Many of these companies had followed Litton's example by purchasing other companies, and Litton's structure was becoming increasingly complex.[12]

Among the scores of acquisitions during that time, Western Geophysical Company of America and Ingalls Shipbuilding Corporation fit into Litton's structure quite well. Unlike many other Litton acquisitions, both went on to become important long-term divisions of the company.

A New Frontier

At the time of its acquisition in 1960, Western Geophysical Company of America had more than 900 employees and $15 million in sales and was the world's largest explorer of the ocean's depths for oil and minerals. Western Geophysical had mapped more of the ocean floor than all other companies in the field combined.[13]

Seismic exploration is done by creating shock waves that are recorded as they reverberate from inside the earth. At that time, the shock waves were generated in a variety of ways, including the use of explosive charges to create small, localized

earthquakes. The result was a composite map of the earth's underground structure, a map that was not just confined to the ocean floor. Western Geophysical then assembled the information in a form tailored to its clients.[14]

The acquisition seemed peculiar on the surface, but Litton's expertise in electronics was tailored to Western Geophysical's need for new, smaller, lighter and more accurate equipment in seismic exploration. In effect, Litton bought a market for itself. By adding its electronics expertise to the seismic exploration skills of Western Geophysical, Litton established something bigger and better than what had previously existed, the very definition of synergy, or another "technological cascade."

Litton applied its technology to Western Geophysical's seismic exploration, thus improving the methods by which oil and minerals were located beneath the ocean.

As Western Geophysical CEO Henry Salvatori pointed out when the acquisition was announced, "In recent years there has been a constantly increasing dependence upon electronics in the field of geophysical research. We feel that the continuing demand for the company's services will be enhanced appreciably by the added scientific talents and electronic experience available to us from the Litton organization."[15]

Characteristically, Thornton saw more than just an enhancement of what already existed. "Oceanography is as challenging as space," he said, "and it may have even greater potential."[16]

Getting Shipshape

In 1961, another large acquisition seemed to range even further afield when Litton bought the troubled Ingalls Shipbuilding Corporation in Pascagoula, Mississippi. "When we bought Ingalls," Thornton said, "a lot of people thought we were pretty crazy, trying to get big for bigness' sake. They didn't see how an old, worn-out industry like shipbuilding made any sense."[17] But it was a classic Litton move: buy a troubled but respected company in an area in which Litton was not involved, use it to establish a new market for Litton products, and combine the two to create something new and better.

Ingalls had begun operations in 1938 and had produced more than 250 vessels of different types, including more than 200 for the U.S. Navy, by the time Litton acquired it. But as a result of a long period of internal problems, Ingalls was losing money. It didn't help that, as *Fortune* magazine noted, shipbuilding in the United States was regarded as "a tired industry in a highly competitive world market and partially dependent on government subsidy."[18]

All of which explained why Ingalls was a steal. Litton acquired a company that had $60 million in annual sales by assuming $9 million of its debt and turning over $8 million of Litton stock.[19] Almost overnight, Litton became the nation's third largest shipbuilder.

Among the many craft that came out of the shipyard were submarines. Ingalls received its first contract to build a nuclear-powered attack submarine in 1958. With the Soviet Union build-ing more submarines than any navy in the world (265 submarines joined the Soviet fleet between 1950 and 1958),[20] detecting the stealthy underwater menace through the use of technologically advanced surface ships and attack submarines became extremely important. In April 1950, a congressional defense committee recommended adding $600 million to defense appropriations.[21] Much of the funding was earmarked for antisubmarine warfare, for both submarines and sub-hunting surface warships such as destroyers and frigates.

Within its first nine months as a Litton division, Ingalls had won contracts to build seven new ships.[22] Under Litton, Ingalls' contracts were extended to amphibious assault ships, cargo ships, oceanography research vessels and oil-drilling vessels.

New Companies, New Products

Western Geophysical and Ingalls Shipbuilding were Litton's two biggest buys in the sixties, and each spurred the company into lucrative markets. But Litton's growth wasn't limited to domestic acquisitions. By 1962, foreign customers accounted for 25 percent of Litton sales.[23]

In 1961, Litton entered the microwave oven market when it signed an agreement with the Tappan Company. In 1965, Litton produced its first marketable microwave ovens, which sold for $1,000 each. Although they were originally meant for commercial use and weren't sold to private consumers for several years, microwave ovens eventually became the Litton product with the highest profile. Unlike navigation systems or submarines, people could have Litton microwaves in their homes. Litton's identification with microwave ovens continued long after it stopped making them when the company's prices were drastically undercut by manufacturers in Korea and Japan.

Aside from the microwave tube, the Electron Tube Division's other developments during the 1960s included a klystron for the Ballistic Missile Early Warning System (BMEWS) — a relatively low-frequency, high-power, over-the-horizon radar for the detection of ballistic missiles — and the L-5120, a high-efficiency, high-average power klystron, for the Los Alamos Meson Physics Facility (LAMPF, now LANSCE) accelerator. The division's L-3408 switch tubes were used as switch regulator elements in the klystron power supplies for the LAMPF linear accelerator. Moreover, the division expanded its product line to include helix traveling wave tubes (TWTs), setting a quantity record for helix TWT with the APS-109 tube.[24]

Another acquisition made in 1961, Cole Steel Equipment, an office furniture manufacturer, helped make Litton's Business Machine Group the nation's fastest growing supplier of office equipment, services and supplies.[25] Once again, Litton's purchase confounded business analysts. Litton's management explained that it was already prominent in business machines, so why not deal in the entire office as one unit?

Litton continued to pursue that strategy when it bought Royal McBee (typewriters and office machines); the A. Kimball Company (point-of-sale tags, tickets and labels, plus a system for the automated ticketing and control of retail inventory); Simon Adhesive Products (adhesives for the backs of labels); and Eureka Specialty (trading stamps, a fad popular in the 1950s and 1960s).

Meanwhile, Litton had the market for inertial guidance systems virtually to itself. In 1961, Litton's

inertial guidance system was the only one operational in the free world's fighter aircraft. Five years later, Litton produced the first guidance system used by commercial aircraft.

Litton's 1961 acquisition of Germany's C. Plath (marine navigation equipment) gave Litton a European plant in which to produce inertial navigation systems for NATO. In 1962, Litton's inertial system was selected for installation in a number of F-4C Phantom IIs, the first operational U.S. Air Force fighters to have such equipment.[26] The LN-3 inertial navigation system was followed by several more sophisticated versions, including the Stellar-Inertial-Doppler System in 1966, first used in the FB-111 Aardvark.

Litton products also played an important role in the Vietnam conflict. The company's inertial systems were on board the A-6 Intruder and the EA version, used for electronic countermeasures and electronic intelligence gathering. The Intruder earned a reputation as a superb all-weather attack jet with first-class operating capabilities under the worst environmental conditions.[27]

Litton Data Systems supported the Navy and Air Force in Vietnam with its carrier-based Airborne Tactical Data Systems (ATDS), which were installed in the Navy's E-2A Hawkeye aircraft. The ATDS gave the Navy its first airborne automated air surveillance and control system and early warning capability for fleet air defense.[28] It was one of the earliest systems to provide "situational awareness" to the operator.[29] And in 1966, Data Systems provided the U.S. Marine Corps with its AN/TYQ-2, the world's most advanced mobile air defense command and control system at that time. This Marine Tactical Data System (MTDS) was used to shorten reaction time in high-speed weapon systems.[30] Litton field representatives (including Darwin Beckel, a corporate vice president and president of Guidance & Control

Left: Litton combined its advanced technology with mass-production efficiency to produce top-quality microwave ovens.

Opposite: Complex electronic instrumentation of Litton Systems Canada in Toronto operated around the clock to test LN-3 inertial navigation systems for NATO aircraft.

The Monrobot XI, which made its debut in 1960, was designed for small businesses that couldn't afford $100,000 or more for a computer.

Systems in 1999) were stationed in Vietnam to assist in training, service and maintenance.[31]

While it stayed away from big general-purpose computers, Litton made a serious move in small computers and became a pioneer in the field. Today the machines look like something out of a 1950s science fiction movie, but they were remarkable at the time. The next model in Litton's Monrobot series, the Monrobot XI, was the smallest business computer on the market, costing about $25,000 in 1962. By the next year, about 200 had been installed (they were particularly popular at brokerage firms and oil companies), and they were being produced at the rate of about 20 per month.[32]

Litton added to its components technology when it purchased Winchester Electronics in 1963. Winchester, which was founded in 1941, already had a strong presence in the field of specialized connectors. In the early 1950s, it had masterminded a unique Rack & Panel connector called MRE, which was designed into the Lockheed F-104 Starfighter

and helped Winchester obtain its first military specification approval (MIL-C-8384). In 1955, the National Aircraft Standards Committee expressed a need for a two-piece printed circuit connector with protective shells, and Winchester engineered its "W" series as a result. The "W" series evolved into the WM line, which was designed into the Titan and other missile programs.[33]

Further strengthening its hold in connectors, Litton purchased VEAM, located in Milan, Italy, in 1967. VEAM had been in operation since 1936 and had been producing and distributing MIL-C-5015 and MIL-C-26482 cylindrical connectors for Bendix, among other products.[34]

Over the 1957-through-1965 period, Litton made various acquisitions that eventually resulted in the Amecom division, then located in Silver Spring and College Park, Maryland. These divisions, which included the Emertron division of Emerson Radio and Maryland Electronics Manufacturing Company (MEMCO), produced antennas and other receiver-type equipment. Amecom, in the mid-1960s, was a manufacturer of diverse electronic equipment including altimeters that were installed on the Air Force's C-5A Galaxy aircraft, simulators like the Alvin Two Man Submarine, IFF antennas for the FAA and antennas used for intelligence gathering.

In addition, Amecom manufactured wideband noise jammers for the military, including the ALT-27. As a result of this jammer activity, Amecom developed a patented technique called the "Binary Beam," which was based upon phase interferometry — that is, measuring the phase difference between a signal received at two or more antennas. This technique yielded a very accurate measure of the signal's angle-of-arrival (AOA), or azimuth, with which to steer the jammer antenna. The Amecom technique was somewhat revolutionary in that it used more antenna/receiver channels than were traditionally used by its competitors but permitted much higher component errors, enabling the use of less expensive components while still achieving precise angular measurements. Thus, Amecom was able to achieve on military platforms (aircraft, ships and submarines) AOA measurements previously only realized in a highly controlled, calibrated laboratory environment.[35]

Small Steps for Mankind

The Apollo moon program was one of the most exciting and nationally unifying adventures in American history. But the giant leap for mankind was made up of a series of small steps — and not just those taken by Neil Armstrong. From Project Mercury to Project Apollo, Litton Industries played a major role in the mission that has become one of the defining moments of the 20th century.

Throughout much of the sixties, Litton was heavily involved in the 12 two-man flights that comprised Project Gemini, which lasted from 1964 to 1967. The project's purpose was to test astronauts' ability to maneuver spacecraft by manual control, a vital precursor to the Apollo moon missions. Each Gemini vehicle relied on more than 100 different Litton components, such as high-temperature antennas that transmitted signals back to earth.

On the ground, Litton supported the space program by building the first space chamber (a vacuum chamber to simulate weightlessness) and the first space suit. Although never used in space, the suit is on display at the Smithsonian Institution. Litton also created a special wind tunnel to simulate space capsule reentry into the atmosphere and built a block-long "moonscape" as a testing ground.[36]

For the historic moon mission itself, Litton's Electron Tube Division designed and built two special 21-inch cathode ray tubes (CRTs) for the Lunar Module Procedure Simulator (LMPS). The CRTs were mounted on the outside of the simulator, a duplicate of the Lunar Excursion Module (LEM) used to land and take off from the moon. The CRTs displayed the lunar landscape as it would appear to the astronauts at an altitude of 50,000 feet. When the astronauts began their "descent," the CRT-generated landscape adjusted accordingly, providing a feeling of reality to the simulation.

The Aero Service division designed a full-color, 6-foot-diameter earth model used in a simulator developed for NASA to give a visual presentation of earth to astronaut trainees "orbiting" in a simulated space capsule. Aero Service also was the sole producer of film graphics to simulate both earth orbits and lunar landing sites as they would be encountered by astronauts. Aero Service artists produced color renditions of eight earth orbits and rendered lunar landing sites as seen from a capsule approaching the moon. These sequential presentations allowed astronauts to actually "fly" the mission from the earth and touch down on the moon. In the spring of 1969, more lunar scenes were produced by Aero Service to train astronauts for *Apollo 11*. By that time, artists had the benefit of real lunar photography to reproduce landing sites in painstaking detail.

Litton engineers Siegfried Hansen (left) and Henry Singleton outside a vacuum chamber at the Space Research Laboratory in Beverly Hills.

Litton's Monroe division manufactured and installed more than 200 calculators at Cape Kennedy, including those used in the Astronaut Training Command for the intricate work involved in the astronauts' simulator time. The Kennedy Space Center's vehicle assembly building also used a number of Monroe calculators to solve the complex problems involved in the assembly of spacecraft and rocket boosters. The Space Center's weights and balances department used these calculators to prepare the spacecraft for launch.

The LC-39 Mobile Service Structure (MSS), a 400-foot tower that stood alongside the *Saturn V* rocket, was built by Litton's Rust Engineering division. The tower, the size of a 40-story building, was one of the largest movable land objects in the world. It included elevators, smaller buildings or work-

rooms, a power plant, sanitary facilities and supporting equipment. The MSS was placed alongside the *Saturn V* to allow technicians to conduct inspections, fueling, final installations and checkout procedures before liftoff.

The Litcom division manufactured and installed cable harnesses, terminal boxes, operational intercom systems and a variety of other elements for the Kennedy Space Center launch complex. Litcom also supported the launches with four weather fax recorders, which received continuous weather data from the United States Weather Bureau and the United States Air Force Weather Transmitting Network.

Litton's Profexray division provided its 300 MA 125 KV Diagnostic X-ray for the Manned Spacecraft Center in Houston, which used it to help certify the astronauts for flight and to check the astronauts' condition upon return. The Potentiometer division manufactured the equipment that controlled the liquid oxygen and hydrogen components of the rocket fuel for the *Saturn V* rocket.

The majority of the bolts and screws used on the Apollo capsules were supplied by the Dumont Aviation division. In recognition of this role, Dumont was presented with a plaque with a bolt taken from *Apollo 11*.

Triad-Utrad manufactured subminiature transformers for the Apollo guidance systems, while Airtron furnished S-band components for use in ground tracking stations for the Apollo lunar program. The Amecom division made four S-band quartz antenna discs attached to the *Apollo 11* Command Service Module. The discs were used for communication with Mission Control at the NASA Manned Spacecraft Center in Houston as backup for the main antenna system. The antennas were also used for live voice; tracking and telemetry information; transmissions such as navigational and biomedical information, including the astronauts' temperatures; oxygen consumption rate; and blood pressures.

The Twin City Tool division manufactured approximately 1,200 bipods for the *Saturn V* J-2 engines. A cluster of six engines was used on the *Saturn V* for each of the Apollo missions, with eight bipods used per launch as part of the engines' linkage controls. The division also manufactured 18 special fittings from blocks of titanium that were part of the housing for the Lunar Excursion Module.

Tracking the Apollo missions demanded a worldwide deployment of stations, some of them at sea on board Navy ships. Three ships were outfitted by Litton's Encoder division, which provided six optical encoders in the flexure monitor equipment. The superstructures of all ships flex at sea, a motion that is imperceptible to the naked eye. The flexing action causes slight errors in determining the exact location of a vehicle in space. To compensate in the Apollo program, the flexing was measured by a laser-optical system in the flexure monitor. The data was translated by the Litton encoders and fed into shipboard computers that correlated it with radar tracking information to give an accurate fix on the space vehicle.

The Poly-Scientific division developed a series of slip ring capsule assemblies for use in the Saturn guidance system. The slip ring assemblies were also used in the flight director altitude indicator in the Apollo cockpit, in the communications

antennas and in the lunar module. Poly-Scientific pioneered the development of new materials, process methods and design to yield the extraordinary reliability required in the Apollo mission. The division also supplied the slip ring assemblies used in the Apollo flight simulator at the Manned Spacecraft Center in Houston.

The Clifton division supplied three multi-speed resolver assemblies, key elements in the inertial guidance system that provided the basic guidance and navigation for the command module. Clifton also supplied precision coordinates for the space sextant and the telescope that permitted astronauts to update and corroborate spacecraft position by taking a fix on the stars.

In the Lunar Receiving Laboratory, where astronauts were quarantined after their flights, the Stouffer Frozen Foods division was called upon for its range of menus and expertise in convenience foods, ultimately providing more than 50 percent of the entrees consumed by the astronauts during quarantine. The Atherton division outfitted the kitchens used during the astronauts' quarantine after the space missions.

Electra Motors manufactured a special 7.5-horsepower motor used to power the grinder through which moon rock samples were passed to break them into test sizes.

Eight drive systems for the launch pads were designed and built by the Louis Allis division. The biggest of these — a 2,500-horsepower Louis Allis adjustable speed drive — controlled the pumping of 1 million gallons of liquid oxygen at the rate of 10,000 gallons per minute.

Perfecting the Image

As Litton acquired more companies and introduced more products, the numbers told a dazzling story. In 1963, Litton had more than $500 million in sales. The next year, it passed $750 million. In 1965, it shot past the $1 billion mark, and only three years after that, Litton passed $2 billion in sales. In 1966, Litton stock sold for 33 times its annual earnings. By comparison, ITT did very well for itself at just about half that amount.

There were other changes too. On September 8, 1961, Thornton relinquished the Litton presidency to Roy Ash, which only confirmed on paper what had already happened in business. Thornton remained as chairman of the board and took on the additional title of chief executive officer.

Three years later, Litton completed a long overdue move to a new corporate address on Santa Monica Boulevard in Beverly Hills. With its fountain, tall white columns, two large spiral staircases and white classical structure, the new headquarters was described as "a stately colonial mansion."[37] It had been built by legendary Hollywood agent Jules Stein.

In terms of public image, Litton Industries had gone decidedly upscale in a very short time. Nothing illustrated that more than its annual reports, described at various times as "magnificently mounted"[38] and having "a greater resemblance to

Purchased from MCA Studios, Litton's new white-pillared company headquarters featured oak-paneled walls, spiral staircases, and a modern theater and projection room.

first-rate auction gallery catalogues than the accountings of major corporations."[39]

The reports were as important for how they looked and the impression they made as for what they said. A great deal of thought was given to the theme, the weight of the paper and the printing quality. The 1964 report was literally a hardcover book, with individual achievement in a free society as the theme. The cover featured a sketch of artist Andrew Wyeth, and each section opened with a sketch and brief biography by such notable achievers as Pulitzer Prize–winning historian Richard Hofstadter and French statesman Jean Monnet.

The 1965 annual report featured full-color reproductions of classic works of art, including a cover reproduction of a portrait by renaissance painter Hans Holbein, chosen because the subject of the painting represented the "spirit which is important to the development of Litton Industries."[40]

The 1966 report featured an essay on "Managing Ideas" by another Pulitzer Prize winner, historian Allan Nevins, while the 1967 edition came with reproductions of art in stained glass. The cover was designed to resemble a stained glass window and included this explanation: "This stained glass window symbolizes the ethics of 15th century commercial life at Tournai, Belgium. The citizen in the purple robe has volunteered to authenticate weights and measures. A shopman is moving a cask on the scale while a clerk records the weight in circles and crosses. The towers embossed on the hexagonal and conical weights are the official mark of the town."[41]

As a final touch, copies of the Litton annual reports were mailed to industry and political leaders in the Soviet Union, where they were said to be very popular.[42]

This triumph of public relations was the brainchild of Crosby Kelly, the crack PR man Thornton had met years earlier at Ford and eventually induced to join Litton. A great deal of the Litton image can be credited to the tireless Kelly, who ran one of the most adroit public relations programs in the nation without seeming to run one at all. Kelly carefully cultivated the Litton aura, with the annual reports as just one example.

"Facts never made a man," he said. "It's men that make facts…. Unless you can reach the minds

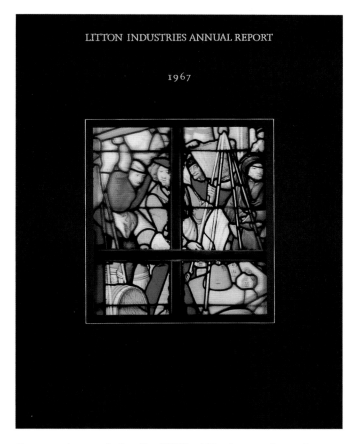

For several years during the 1960s, Litton's annual reports were literal works of art. The cover of the 1967 report, for example, featured a thick canvas cover set over a translucent painting — much like a stained-glass window.

of the people, don't bother me with the facts. I tell people I'm a confidence man and I make no apologies for it…. People respond to non-logical things."[43]

The Making of Men

Kelly nurtured Thornton's image as the cowboy capitalist and created a cult of personality around him. Thornton was seen as a man who lived the life of a multimillionaire entrepreneur and yet somehow disdained it at the same time. When Thornton learned to fly and bought a twin-engine Aero Commander, that, too, became part of his persona. Thornton bought a 230-acre Southern California ranch, cementing the cowboy image. Virtually all of the magazine stories

The media liked to feature Thornton as a "tough trail boss," a man who saddled up to get away from it all at his San Fernando Valley ranch.

included details of how he saddled up his favorite horse, Prince, before daylight, then rode into the mountains with a packed lunch, water, a first-aid kit and a revolver to blow away rattlesnakes.

In the meantime, Ash was presented as a human computer and financial genius who was the number cruncher behind Thornton's vision and salesmanship. According to one Litton executive, Thornton and Ash could run any company independently, but put together, they created "a new dimension."[44]

The stories were not entirely true, but as image-making goes, they were a success. In its cover story on Litton Industries (a business-related cover story was rare at the time), *Time* stated that Thornton may be "the best executive in the U.S. today."[45] Long after Thornton's death, Fenimore declared that John Wayne was the only actor he could think of who could have played Thornton in a movie based on Thornton's life.[46]

A One-Rule Company

Not every move Litton made was a success, but the successes dwarfed the mistakes. Litton flopped when it got into the surplus U.S. Army tank-engine business. The company wrote off the venture as an inventory loss. Later, Litton bought Stouffer Foods in 1967 for almost $100 million in Litton stock. The rationale behind this acquisition was that Stouffer's frozen foods fit perfectly with Litton's microwave ovens. The Stouffer acquisition also got Litton into the hotel and restaurant business, which was never particularly successful, while the Litton microwave–Stouffer's frozen food synergy never developed because any company's frozen food could go into a microwave. Even after being acquired by Litton, Stouffer was reluctant to make the expensive conversion from aluminum (which cannot be used in a microwave) to paper containers. Litton sold Stouffer to Nestlé Foods for $105 million in 1973, when Litton was plagued by severe financial problems.

But even then, the Stouffer deal wasn't viewed as a mistake. Rather, Litton was thought to have been too farsighted. "We were probably about 10 years or so ahead of our time," Ash said, almost 20 years after the acquisition.[47]

Litton's corporate style — lean, nimble and resolutely informal — governed this vast indus-

trial empire without what was scornfully referred to as the "palace guard" that dulled the reflexes of other corporations. This culture created a seedbed of executive talent, spawning what Litton people proudly refer to as LIDOs (Litton Industries Dropouts). Ash explained the company's secret for nurturing talent to *Business Week* magazine in 1966: "We have one rule ... there is no rule."[48]

As of 1966, Litton Industries had five groups — Business Equipment, Industrial and Professional, Defense and Space, Components, and Transportation Systems — and 59 divisions scattered within those groups. A vice president was in charge of each group, but as long as they met financial projections, division managers were generally free to run the companies as their own. Those projections were aggressive, however. Litton generally demanded a substantial return on a division's gross assets. Controls were tight financially but loose almost everywhere else, and the result was a remarkable esprit de corps.[49]

"Litton brought a lot of good people together and gave them their heads," said one Litton executive. "They let you take off by yourself, and they didn't look over your shoulder."[50]

Or, as future CEO Fred O'Green told *Business Week* in 1966, "Father Litton creates the environment and leaves us free to use all our energies in new and creative ways."[51]

Fast on the Draw

Thanks to a "lack of reverence for the classical trappings of corporate life,"[52] the Litton style was light on memos and long on personal contact, for as Litton executives were fond of saying, "You can't put a smile or a shrug in a memo."[53] Although offices were equipped with "squawk boxes" that allowed managers to talk to each other without leaving their chairs, a manager could easily and informally drop in on his boss to discuss a business issue and maybe even solve the problem while leaning in the office doorway. Ash once said personal contact was vital because "you can't debate very well on paper."[54]

Litton executives might make a dozen long-distance telephone calls within an hour, then fly cross-country at a moment's notice. They used "coast-to-coast jets like taxicabs"[55] and spent so

LITTON INDUSTRIES DROPOUTS

SINCE ITS FOUNDING IN 1953, LITTON Industries has attracted some of the nation's best business executives. But as anyone who has ever run a successful corporation knows, top-notch teams do not tend to stay together very long. Ambition may drive one executive to become a CEO in his own right. Another may get an offer that's too good to refuse. And there are always valuable executives who find they are hitting their heads on the corporate ceiling.

Over its history, Litton has had so many executives go on to become presidents, chairmen, or top officers of other large companies that they became known as LIDOs (Litton Industries Dropouts), although longtime Litton President Roy Ash suggested, "They really should be called 'Ligrads,' because they were graduated from the Litton Industries executive finishing school."[1]

"Our aim is to man the company with entrepreneurial people," Ash told *Business Week* in 1967. "Truly, if we are going to get that kind of people, we have to give them continual opportunity for themselves, upward mobility to express their own self-confidence and independence — even if it means some will have to leave Litton for their ultimate fulfillment."[2]

Even Ash himself became a LIDO, initially as director of the Office of Management and Budget during the Nixon administration and later as chairman and CEO of Addressograph-Multigraph.

The width and breadth of the LIDO list is impressive, and it is one in which Litton takes considerable pride. "I don't think any other company has had the kind of talent we've had," said retired Chairman, President and CEO John Leonis in a 1998 interview. "Whatever caused these LIDOs, that was something unique to Litton."[3]

Litton Executive	Company Headed and/or Founded
Harry J. Gray	United Technologies Corp.
Henry Singleton	Teledyne
George Kozmetsky	Teledyne
Fred R. Sullivan	Walter Kidde
George T. Scharffenberger	City Investing
Orion Hoch	Advanced Memory Systems
Ralph H. O'Brien	Mohawk Data Sciences
Gordon MacKenzie	Victor Comptometer
Frank Ricciardi	Richton International
William E. McKenna	Hunt Foods
William George	Medtronic
Russell McFall	Western Union
James McMahan	Baker Industries
James Mellor	General Dynamics
Joseph Smead	Kaiser Electronics
Frank Moothart	Republic Corp.
Seymour Rosenberg	Mattel
Fred Mayor	American Export

much time on the telephone that, according to one estimate, the annual telephone bill for corporate headquarters was $7 million in the mid-1960s.[56]

The result was an extraordinarily fast-moving company, one that was renowned for its ability to make a deal before its competitors knew that there was a deal to be made.

In one example, within two and one-half hours after the chance arose, Litton decided to buy Hewitt-Robins, Inc., a venerable Connecticut-based company that specialized in bulk materials-handling equipment and had annual sales in excess of $50 million.[57]

Once he learned that the acquisition was possible, Ash flew overnight from Los Angeles to Stamford, Connecticut. After meeting with executives from Hewitt-Robins, he held an executive committee meeting over the telephone with Thornton in Texas and Senior Vice President Glen McDaniel in Los Angeles. They decided on an offering price, and Ash began negotiations with Hewitt-Robins. The next day, after breakfast, he attended a special Hewitt-Robins weekend board meeting and cut the deal.

A few months later, in January 1966, Litton added the Alvey-Ferguson Company, which manufactured computer-controlled warehouse unit handling systems, to complement the equipment built by Hewitt-Robins — yet another example of "technological cascade."

Nearing the end of the decade, Litton Industries was one of the wonder companies of the age or, as Fenimore said, "a model of entrepreneurship in the postwar era."[58]

Over it all, Litton exuded a strong sense of self-satisfaction. "The race is to the quick, and no one is quicker than Litton," said Ash. "It is a heady experience for those who can stand it."[59]

The Pascagoula River reflects the brilliant lights of Litton's Ingalls shipyard.

CHAPTER FIVE

WAKING FROM THE DREAM

1967–1972

"Many people were second-guessing the wisdom of our rapid expansion and diversification. But I personally believe Litton would be an extremely different — and probably far lesser — company today without our opportunistic, rapid expansion phase in the sixties."

— Fred O'Green, 1988[1]

AS THE 1960s BEGAN TO WIND down, the future of Litton Industries looked as bright as its past. The world's best-known and most successful conglomerate had soared like a rocket from its beginnings as a small microwave tube manufacturer.

By the late 1960s, Litton stock was selling at more than $120 a share, or almost 50 times its earnings. Its market value of $2.7 billion put it on par with some of the nation's largest and most venerable corporations such as General Motors and Goodyear.

An Absentee Landlord

Speculation swirled that Thornton might succeed longtime friend and fellow Whiz Kid Robert McNamara as secretary of defense. The speculation had its roots in Thornton's expertise in national defense issues, not surprising since so much of Litton's business was in national defense. Other factors that made such an appointment seem logical included Thornton's long friendship with McNamara and his familiarity with Vietnam and the war in Southeast Asia.

Speculation notwithstanding, at Litton's annual meeting in 1967 Thornton flatly denied that he intended to resign, stating bluntly, "I have no plans to leave Litton."[2] Still, there was no denying that he was spending a great deal of his time in activities outside of Litton Industries. Thornton sat on the boards of eight other companies and two colleges and was an active trustee of the University of Southern California. He also served on a variety of other government panels, boards and groups, including President Lyndon Johnson's National Advisory Commission on Civil Disorders and an investigation of a cheating scandal at the Air Force Academy.

Gradually, Thornton was delegating more of the responsibility of running Litton to Roy Ash, and it grew clear that Ash by himself wasn't nearly as effective as Thornton and Ash together. Ash simply was not as well liked as Thornton. Ash was cool; Thornton was warm. Ash worked numbers; Thornton worked with people. Ash had procedures; Thornton had insight. Thornton himself recognized the problem. Although he took pride in his outside work, he later admitted, "I was getting away from my first love, Litton."[3]

Modular Success

Even as Thornton pulled himself further from the company's daily operations, Litton continued to look ahead. In January 1968, the company began constructing an innovative new shipbuilding facility on a 611-acre site across the Pascagoula River from the existing Ingalls shipyard.

The new shipyard featured modular production techniques, a new manufacturing concept in the United States. Traditionally, ships had been built from the keel up on an inclined shipway. The completed ship slid down the inclined way into the water. The modular system, by contrast, divided a ship into "modules" manufactured on an assembly-line basis, similar to automobile manufacturing. Modular shipbuilding allowed pre-outfitting of the interior prior to the final joining of the sections to form the hull. Originally developed in Sweden, modular construction is faster and less expensive than traditional from-the-keel-up shipbuilding, although it had never been tried on the scale envisioned by Litton.

In a 1998 interview, Ingalls Vice President Den Knecht explained the advantages of modular ship construction over traditional construction.

"On a traditional, inclined shipway, you're limited both to the size of the ship and its weight.... You ended up launching the ship 40 to 45 percent complete, then tying it up to a dock in the water. Only then could the heavy equipment be installed, but that required going through the corridors of the ship to put in piping, electrical work, ventilation, etc. It was very labor-intensive work compared to modular construction.

"With modular construction, we build the ship in vertical sections. We leave the sections open until very late in the project so that we have easy access to all portions of the ship. Most important, we build the sections of the ship, and we completely outfit those sections as we're building them."[4]

The shipyard went into production in 1970. Workers laid the keel for its first vessel — the SS *Austral Envoy*, a commercial cargo container ship. Altogether there were four such ships on order, but this was the first to be built at Litton's shipyards using modular production.

The SS *Austral Envoy*, a commercial cargo container ship, was the first to be built at Litton's shipyards using modular construction.

A Hard Blow

With its stock soaring, its earnings rising and its reputation impeccable, Litton was the standard to which many other corporations aspired. The first sign that something might be wrong came when, for the first time in its history, Litton presented bad news to its shareholders. On January 22, 1968, a letter went out to shareholders reporting that Litton's profits for the fiscal quarter ending January 31 were "substantially" lower than expected, thus ending 57 consecutive quarters of earnings gains. This was mainly due to unexpected losses in the Business Equipment Group.[5]

It was the first setback in Litton history, although as Ash pointed out, profits had not ceased. Litton attributed the decline to "certain earlier deficiencies of management personnel" — a phrase that would haunt Litton for years. What was intended as a forthright explanation from Ash and Thornton — who were, after all, the key "management personnel" — was interpreted by many inside and outside the company as an attempt to place the blame elsewhere.[6] This was stunning news from a corporation that bragged about how its managers could, and certainly seemed to, manage any company in any industry.

Litton stock fell 18 points within a week. Then it tumbled to little more than half of what it sold for only a few weeks earlier (although it did recover some of the loss through the rest of the year).

The reaction on Wall Street seemed out of proportion to the event, for as Ash pointed out, profits continued to flow into the company, which operated under the same managers who were performing the same procedures they had six weeks earlier.

One theory for the panic stems from the notion that the stock market is as much about perception as it is about reality. Many analysts thought that Litton was overvalued and had to return to earth at some point. Even Ash agreed. In an interview years later, he claimed that both he and Thornton knew the stock was priced too high.

"No matter what we did, there was no possible way to get the earnings to justify the price," he said. "People were buying at huge multiples because they assumed a level of sales and earnings that was impossible to obtain. The question at the time was,

are we obligated to tell our shareholders that the price of the stock was totally unjustified. We decided against it."[7]

Also, more than a few people were waiting for the company to stumble and took pleasure when it did because Litton's remarkable rise engendered a lot of envy. According to an article in *Fortune* magazine titled "Litton Down to Earth," cynics of conglomerates in general were joined by officers of other conglomerates in thinking that any company that came so far in such a short time had to be more smoke and mirrors than substance.[8] What at another corporation might have been shrugged off as something bound to happen sooner or later was regarded as a major failure simply because it was Litton Industries.[9]

Add to this the extraordinarily complex structure of the company, its range of products and its size — by then about 120,000 employees — and the Litton landscape suddenly seemed littered with problems.

The success of Litton, like other corporations, tends to reflect what is happening in the country at any given time, and 1968 was one of America's most turbulent years since the Civil War. The conflict in Vietnam was ripping the country apart as opposition to the war grew. Martin Luther King Jr. was murdered in April, and two months later, Robert F. Kennedy was assassinated. Protest and violence marred the Democratic National Convention in Chicago, and race riots flared in more than 60 cities during what was called the "long, hot summer."

Within Litton itself, a lack of cash flow and capital resources throughout the company led to cutbacks elsewhere. For example, Litton's efforts to convert business equipment from electromechanical to electronic had to be suspended due to lack of funds for research and development.[10] The return on sales in typewriters, copying machines, calculators and cash registers was only 3 percent, compared to the 12.6 percent return for industry leader IBM and an industry average of 7 percent. Litton's Royal typewriters lost $6.5 million in one year, and its market share in copying machines was just 1 percent.[11] Moreover, Litton suffered from its own high expectations, for sustaining impressive gains in earnings becomes harder when a corporation is worth several billion dollars.

In a speech several years later, Fred O'Green, who succeeded Ash as president, put what the company went through in historical context: "Many people were second-guessing the wisdom of our rapid expansion and diversification. But I personally believe that Litton would be an extremely different — and probably far lesser — company today without our opportunistic, rapid expansion phase in the sixties."[12]

Still, Litton struggled to make coherence out of 25 product lines grouped into 17 major product divisions and labored to stabilize growth versus earnings. Earnings of about $70 million in 1967 fell to $58 million the following year, only to bounce back to $82 million in 1969 (much of that due to acquisitions). The next year, with total sales approaching $2.4 billion, earnings tumbled to $68.7 million,[13] and stock fell to $14 a share, then to $6 in 1973 and to less than $3 in 1974, when Litton posted a loss of $48 million.[14]

Litton Industries did not suffer alone. The country reeled from a recession and high interest rates (reaching at one point near 20 percent), the oil embargo, wage and price controls, and labor unrest.

DIAMOND IN THE ROUGH

THOUGH THE TRANSITION FROM THE 1960s to the 1970s proved to be a rough time for Litton Industries, many of the individual divisions were making thrilling new discoveries, inventing products that would stay with Litton for years to come. One such treasure had already been unearthed at Litton's Airtron division — a crystal made from rare earths heated at intensely high temperatures, a crystal that would be hailed as the world's most popular low-cost synthetic diamond.[1]

In the mid-1960s, Airtron began growing single-crystal yttrium aluminum garnets (YAGs) for laser applications. A young engineer named Donald Lepore, who later became president of Airtron and a senior vice president of Litton, began making a substitute for diamonds by growing undoped YAG, which resulted in a clear crystal. The new substance had sufficient hardness and dispersion to simulate a diamond, but it lacked brilliance. It wasn't until Lepore hooked up with a gemologist named Jerry Call, who helped Lepore facet, finish and polish the crystals, that the YAG took on the appearance of a genuine diamond.[2]

As fate would have it, Call happened to be wearing one of the simulated diamonds in a tie tack when he met the vice president of Saks Fifth Avenue at a party. The vice president took notice of the synthetic diamond, and shortly after, in October 1969, Airtron and Saks launched a national campaign to introduce "Diamonair" — a name combining "diamond" with "Airtron" — throughout the 22 branches of Saks Fifth Avenue.

Diamonair became the world's most successful synthetic diamond, predating the cubic zirconia by several years. "The other materials used before fell way short," said Lepore. "You needed something that was harder than glass or stone or concrete, and none of the other materials were hard enough."[3]

So closely did the Diamonair stones resemble genuine diamonds that many people couldn't tell them apart. Even Elizabeth Taylor wore a Diamonair replica of the famous diamond Richard Burton had given her — a million-dollar, 69-carat gem — to thwart potential jewel thieves and to avoid paying the high insurance costs related to wearing such an expensive stone.[4] The Diamonair replica was a huge success, and the story gained national attention in the media.

"The world economy changed drastically in the early seventies," O'Green said. "Inflation spiraled, and money became tighter and more expensive. The United States suffered from excessive government control, export restrictions and costly labor increases."[15]

Total Package Procurement

In the meantime, Litton embarked on an ambitious shipbuilding program. In 1969, Litton had won a contract to build nine Landing Helicopter Assault (LHA) ships. These huge ships, similar to aircraft carriers in size and appearance, are used to transport and land assault troops and supporting equipment by helicopter and landing craft. The ships have a full helicopter deck and a large interior well deck that, when partially flooded, permits the rapid entry and exit of landing craft from the stern.

A year later, Litton landed "the largest single contract in the annals of American shipbuilding,"[16] $2.1 billion for 30 Navy Spruance-class destroyers, which were to be built simultaneously

---

Those who knew they had a synthetic diamond were sometimes fooled too, as was the case when an elderly woman purchased a Diamonair ring as a stand-in for her genuine diamond. After the woman's husband insisted that she wear only her real stone, she decided to return the stand-in. But the Diamonair looked so real that she accidentally returned the genuine diamond ring instead. The sales clerk, not detecting the difference, placed the real diamond in the sales case, and shortly after, it was purchased by a couple who thought they were buying a Diamonair. As luck would have it, they left the ring with the store to be sized, and that night, one of the jewelry buyers was astonished to discover that what was supposed to be a Diamonair ring was actually set with a genuine diamond.[5]

That's when Lepore received a frantic phone call requesting that he make a matching

Diamonair ring before morning. It was a frenzied evening for Lepore and his team, but they succeeded, and the couple picked up their ring the next morning, oblivious that they had almost received the bargain of a lifetime.

By 1971, Zsa Zsa Gabor was promoting Diamonair on television as well as in print ads, and the brand had branched into several fine department stores. It even got attention from *National Geographic.* The magazine compared synthetic diamonds to the real thing, saluting Diamonair's YAG as the hardest and most popular of the low-cost imitations.[6]

Diamonair jewels were being made with cubic zirconia rather than YAG by the mid-1970s because of the higher index of refraction in cubic zirconias. Airtron kept the Diamonair group until 1996, when it was sold to D.G. Jewelry of Canada. But Litton Industries would forever be recognized for having introduced the first truly diamondlike YAG. "There were other companies inventing synthetic diamonds at that time," Lepore said, "but to really make them useful, you have to commercialize them. Airtron, I'm proud to say, was a pioneer in that regard."[7]

Several celebrities served as spokespeople or models for Airtron's Diamonair line of jewelry, including Zsa Zsa Gabor and Lucie Arnaz (above).

Once Ingalls proved how effective modular construction was, other U.S. shipyards began implementing the technique — building ships on an assembly-line basis.

with the LHAs but on separate manufacturing lines. Armed with guided missiles, guns and antisubmarine weaponry, these multimission ships also carry helicopters to extend the fleet's defense and attack capability. Deliveries were scheduled to start in 1974 and extend at least until 1978.

Put together, the two contracts came to more than $3 billion. They represented a new approach called Total Package Procurement, in which the contractor was given total responsibility for the design, construction and fleet readiness under a fixed-price incentive-fee contract. This approach would later prove to be a recipe for disaster.

Finding a Cure

It soon became clear that Litton Industries needed some fundamental changes. Rightly or wrongly, much of the blame fell on Ash. The board and the stockholders were unhappy, especially the previous owners of businesses that Litton had acquired using Litton stock, which was now worth only a fraction of its value when the deals were made.

Then Ash got a timely offer to join the Nixon administration to run the Office of Management and Budget. Ash's last official appearance as president of Litton was at the company's shareholders meeting on December 10, 1972.

Thornton's choice to succeed Ash met with universal approval. Fred O'Green had virtually nothing in common with Roy Ash except that they were both employed by Litton Industries. Thornton remained as chairman and chief executive officer, while O'Green took over as president and chief operating officer.

O'Green was known as an operations man, a friendly, down-to-earth executive who knew how things worked. His past at Litton included directing the highly successful Guidance and Control division, then leading the Defense and Marine Systems group, which included improving the much-troubled shipyard, mainly by joining the two separately operated shipyards into one. O'Green was the kind of man who got involved. "He taught us how to believe in ourselves," remembered Jerry St. Pé,

After Roy Ash retired in December 1972, Thornton (left) and the board of directors chose Fred O'Green (right) to be the new Litton president and COO.

executive vice president and COO of the Litton Ship Systems group.[17]

While conceding that Litton had a lot of "top people," who are "able, dedicated and shrewd," a December 1969 article in *Forbes* magazine summed up the company's problems: "The age of the magic numbers, of blind faith in corporate rhetoric is over, and the time has returned when investors are going to ask about typewriters and machine tools and frozen dinners instead of simply being mesmerized by earnings curves."[18]

In Fred O'Green, whose job was basically to turn the entire corporation around, Litton had a man who knew all about those things and more. O'Green was just what Litton Industries needed — the cure for what ailed it.

The *Ticonderoga,* first in the CG-47 class of Aegis guided missile cruisers, demonstrates her ability to carry out her mission during successful sea trials and weapons testing.

CHAPTER SIX

ALL THE RIGHT MOVES

1973–1981

"What makes the company [Litton] unusual is that it was able to turn around and rise to the heights again. Now, after a lot of radical changes, it is once more sound — a rejuvenated company, better positioned for the struggle to stay on top."

— *Fortune* magazine, 1979[1]

THE DECADE OF THE SEVENTIES presented a difficult time for the American economy and businesses in general. The beginnings of the Watergate scandal, the growing conflict in Vietnam and the often violent reaction to the civil rights movement had already soured the country's mood. Then, in 1973, Egypt and Syria launched a massive offensive against Israel.[2]

Following weeks of desperate fighting, the United States airlifted $2 billion in aid to counter the Soviet Union's support of the Arab nations. Incensed, the Organization of Petroleum Exporting Countries (OPEC) united behind Saudi Arabia on October 20, 1973, in a complete embargo of oil supplies to the United States.[3]

The resulting energy crisis forced conservation to the top of the national agenda. Unable to withstand the pressure, the country plunged into a recession, suffering from a unique climate of rising inflation and recession.[4] From 1973 to 1974, consumer prices rose 12.2 percent and continued to rise until 1978.[5]

Potpourri

While the economy floundered, Litton Industries was still recovering from its stock plunge in 1968 and still trying to tie together the diverse divisions of the company.

With Roy Ash's departure, the top management in 1973 consisted of Tex Thornton (chairman and CEO), Fred O'Green (president and chief operating officer), Glen McDaniel (chairman of the executive committee), and senior vice presidents Joseph T. Casey, Ludwig T. Smith and Crosby M. Kelly.

Litton Industries was a fantastically complex organization. Four product groups had oversight over the divisions, many of them with startling independence. Glen McDaniel noted that it was fashionable among journalists at the time to exaggerate Litton's complexity. Indeed, Litton was then at the height of its diversity and complexity, but the company was well on its way to solving any problems by the time O'Green took over as president. Many of Litton's developments at this time in engineering, production and marketing were no less than monumental.[6]

Run by Executive Vice President Ralph O'Brien and Senior Vice President Orion Hoch, the Business Systems and Equipment group consisted of business systems and equipment, retail and revenue systems, typewriters and office

---

Called the "architect of Litton's recovery effort," Fred O'Green was largely responsible for Litton's restructuring in the 1970s.

copiers, specialty paper, printing and forms, and business furnishing and fixtures.

The Monroe division, part of the Business Systems and Equipment group, was heavily in the calculator business, with 40 different models, and had recently introduced the Monroe 200, an electronic billing system. In Nuremberg, Germany, Triumph-Adler was in the calculator business too, among other endeavors, as was Royal-Imperial.

Other Litton divisions within this group were in the "mini-computer," or desktop computer, field. Sweda was struggling in the cash register business, although Litton had high hopes for the new Cashmark II, a register with only 650 parts, compared to 3,000 parts in a conventional model. In addition, there were lines of portable electric typewriters, office furniture, specialty paper and business forms.

Senior Vice President James Mellor ran the Defense Systems divisions, while Ned Marandino, another senior vice president, directed the group's Marine Systems operations. Together, these two segments comprised the Defense and Marine Systems group, which consisted of navigation and control systems, communications and electronic data systems, and marine engineering and production.

Litton was a leading producer of command and control (C^2) and electronic reconnaissance systems and was easily the world leader in inertial guidance. By 1969, Amecom's patented Binary Beam precision angle-of-arrival (AOA) measurement technique to steer jammer antenna had won the division its first major electronic warfare system, the Passive Detection System (PDS) for the Navy's E-2C early warning aircraft. The system was originally designated the ALR-59 and, following improvements, the ALR-73. The E-2C aircraft also employed other Litton equipment, including Data Systems division's L304 central processor and Guidance and Control's CAINS navigation system.

As a result of the revolutionary Binary Beam technique, Amecom won a number of key passive electronic warfare programs, including the ALQ-124 Adaptive Jammer for the Navy's Fleet EW System Instrumentation Group, the ALQ-25 Tactical Electronic Reconnaissance (TEREC) system for the Air Force's RF-4C aircraft, the

Electronic Support Measures (ESM) system for the Navy's Patrol Hydrofoil Missile (PHM) craft, the ESM system for the Navy's DD-963 Spruance-class destroyer, and the BLD-1 Interferometer Direction Finding System (IDFS) for the Navy's Class 688 submarines.

These passive electronic systems differed from the radar warning receivers manufactured by Litton's Applied Technology division. The radar warning receiver systems were point defense, protecting only the aircraft, while the ESM systems, such as that on the E-2C aircraft, were area defense, protecting a large geographic area. These systems could detect weaker signals emanating from the radar antenna's sidelobes at distant ranges and make very precise measurements of the radar parameters. This yielded very reliable signal identification and precision AOA measurements from which, over time, the radar's geographic location could be determined.[7]

In the new world of the "electronic battlefield," the Data Systems division offered three major systems. TACFIRE was the U.S. Army's first automated field artillery system[8] (and also included the first use of Winchester Electronics' backpanel).[9] The AN/TSQ-73 Missile Minder was a mobile, fully automated missile C^2 system that could coordinate multiple air defense batteries. This was the first automated surface-to-air missile air defense system and was integrated by the U.S. Army into the *Hawk* missile system.[10] Finally, Data Systems' tactical operations systems automated "the processing of combat operations and intelligence data," according to the company's annual report.[11]

Data Systems provided the electronics for the Navy's Landing Helicopter Assault (LHA) class ships and the Spruance-class (DD-963) destroyers, both of which were built at Litton's Ingalls shipyard in Pascagoula. Data Systems designed and integrated the complete combat system for the destroyers and the entire electronics suite on the LHAs.[12] Guidance and Control outfitted the DD-963 destroyers with automated propulsion and steering control systems and provided navigation systems for aircraft that included the Air Force's F-15 Eagle and B-1 Lancer and the Navy's F-14 Tomcat, E-2C Hawkeye and S-3A Viking.

Litton's Carrier Aircraft Inertial Navigation systems "had become standard equipment for carrier-based aircraft," according to the company's annual report.[13] Aero Products supplied navigation systems to commercial airliners all over the world, including the Concorde. Air Force One was another high-profile customer.

Almost 20 percent of Litton's defense sales were outside the country,[14] including MK-I navigation systems to the Canadian Ministry of Transport for short-takeoff-and-landing aircraft, navigation systems for the F-4 Phantom II squadrons of the West German Air Force and electronic subsystems for NATO hydrofoil ships. In addition, LITEF and Litton Italia supplied the main computer, the attitude heading reference unit, the emitter location processor and data communications devices for the European Tornado.

In addition to the LHAs and destroyers, Ingalls had delivered 10 Navy ships and five commercial container ships in the preceding year.

The Industrial Systems and Equipment group included the Machine Tools divisions, led by Senior Vice President Burnell Gustafson, and Component Products and Industrial Systems, headed by Senior Vice President Arnold Kaufman. The group made products for the automotive, aircraft, farm machinery and metal-working industries. It also was involved in "computer-controlled and computer-monitored tools,"[15] including machine tools from Landis Tool that made camshafts and crankshafts for Ford Motor Company. Landis also sold grinding machines for Japanese automobile manufacturers to make rotors for the rotary engines that were popular in the 1970s, with Mazda the best-known example.

Winchester Electronic's Flex-Com IDC connectors — a massive and complete system of connectors, cable and tooling — was gaining attention for its labor-saving capabilities. And the division's patented C-Press® connector line increased its presence in the telecommunications and computer markets.

VEAM Worldwide, meanwhile, had offices in Italy, the United States, Germany and Scotland and was enjoying the U.S. success of its uniquely

The huge LHAs transported and landed assault troops and equipment by helicopter and landing craft.

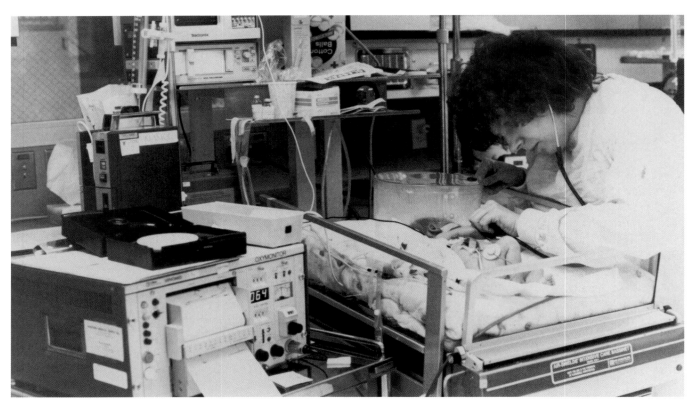

designed quarter-turn, rugged bayonet-lock power connectors.[16]

The Hand Tools division sold products under the Husky, Blackhawk, Spartan and Mustang brand names. Contromatics had recently introduced a valve (the Contro-Seal) that was popular in the chemical, shipbuilding and nuclear-power industries.

Business was good in the magnetic, computer and servo components used in televisions, household appliances, computers, light fixtures and aircraft instruments. Litton made these products in Mexico, Canada, Singapore, Italy and Germany. It also recently had expanded production at its circuit board plant in Springfield, Missouri.

The Electron Tube Division continued to push the technology envelope, developing a highly efficient 200-watt space tube for the Canadian Technology Satellite, which enabled direct broadcast to remote regions all over Canada. This tube included a 10-stage depressed collector that radiated its heat directly into space.[17]

A new product, the Compulift warning system, alerted crane operators when they approached maximum load and boom-angle limits. Louis Allis

Litton's Professional Services and Equipment group produced products such as the Oxymonitor, which told intensive care nurses when to discontinue oxygen therapy to critical infants.

made electric motors, drive systems and digital control equipment. Hewitt-Robins produced bulk handling systems and equipment such as the new Mineveyor that carried coal from the "seam to an outbound conveyor"[18] in coal mines, and its precision gear systems were used during the Vietnam War in helicopters and jet aircraft engines. Litton also sold automatic-mail-handling equipment to the U.S. Postal Service.

Executive Vice President Joseph Imirie was in charge of Litton's last product group, the Professional Services and Equipment group, which included Litton's products that were not identifiable with the other groups: microwave cooking, dental and health care, energy resource exploration, geographical mapping, cancer research, medical and electronic products, educational and professional publishing, and resource exploration.

Western Geophysical, Litton's seismic exploration division, had 60 land and marine crews operating in 21 countries. Aero Service had just completed the "largest and most complex mapping project ever undertaken," 1.7 million square miles of the Amazon jungle.[19] In Freiburg, Germany, Hellige manufactured medical diagnostic and intensive care systems. Profexray was in the X-ray machinery and supplies business and worked with the Eureka X-ray Tube division to develop a dental X-ray for the Dental Products division, which itself had recently come up with an ultrasonic teeth-cleaning device.

In 1973, the National Cancer Institute renewed Bionetics' contract to manage the Frederick Cancer Research Center in suburban Washington, D.C. The Litton Educational Publishing division published books for elementary and high schools, while the Litton Publications division published more than 20 controlled-circulation magazines for the medical profession, chemists, engineers, architects and airline executives.

Background of a Leader

All told, Litton Industries in 1973 was made up of a wide array of products. Litton's operations included 220 "major plants" and 1,324 sales and service centers employing more than 105,000 people around the world.[20]

While its 1973 annual report boasted of Litton's "broad range of divisions and product lines,"[21] Litton's new president and COO, Fred O'Green, was determined to whittle the company down to a more manageable configuration by changing not only what it did, but how it did it. O'Green's plan of action was threefold: tighten the reins on managers so they could detect and deal with potential problems; divest those businesses that strayed from technology; and share knowledge among divisions.[22]

Called "the architect of Litton's recovery effort" by *Business Week* magazine,[23] Fred O'Green was born March 25, 1921, in Mason City, Iowa. Although the name sounds and looks Irish, it is actually Swedish in origin. As often happened during the great waves of immigration into the United States, when O'Green's grandparents came to the United States, impatient immigration officials at

Ellis Island changed the family name from the unfamiliar Ogren to O'Green.

He worked his way through Iowa State University by playing the clarinet at dances and concerts. Concluding that he would never make the top rank of musicians, O'Green considered medicine but couldn't afford the lengthy schooling. Instead, he opted for engineering, earning his degree in electrical engineering in 1943.

Two days after graduation, he married his high school sweetheart, Mildred, and they moved to Washington, D.C., for his new job as electrical engineer at the U.S. Naval Ordnance Laboratory. In 1949, he earned a master's degree in electrical engineering from the University of Maryland.

In a reference to Thornton's storied background at Ford, *Fortune* magazine described O'Green as "something of a whiz kid himself."[24] He helped develop weaponry at the Naval Ordnance Laboratory, then became technical director of space programs at Lockheed Missiles & Space Company, where he was a key figure in accelerating the efforts of the U.S. space program following the near panic that America was losing the "space race" when the Soviet Union launched the *Sputnik* satellite.

O'Green joined Litton in 1962 to run its signature division, Guidance and Control, and his rise was rapid: head of defense and space in 1966, elected to the board in 1968, president in 1972.

Approachable, craggy-faced, and with a thick shock of hair grown long in part to conceal a hearing aid, O'Green was an operations man who knew how things worked, a marked contrast to his predecessor, Ash, and to Thornton, whose strengths were in other areas. O'Green was seen as "down to earth," with a sense of humor that Litton managers found refreshing.

On O'Green's office desk, visitors were greeted with a plaque that read, "I know you believe you understand what you think I said, but I am not sure you realize that what you heard is not what I meant." A two-foot hypodermic syringe sat on his conference table with a plate that read, "The Ultimate Executive Incentive Program."

"Fred O'Green gave us a wonderful environment to be in, where we could really build our own skills and our own competencies," said Nancy Gaymon, corporate vice president, human resources. "He would always say to us, 'I'll give you enough rope to do your job or to hang yourself.' "[25]

O'Green inspired gifts from those who worked for him, one sign of a popular executive. In 1979, after a series of meetings in Hartford, Connecticut, followed by dinner for 22 Litton executives, O'Green was surprised with a unique gift, a chess set with chrome pieces crafted from metal parts made from Litton's Hand Tools division.

As the smiling executives gathered around, O'Green read from a plate on the ornate gift: "You know all the right moves, Fred."

And he did, although the transformation of Litton Industries was not without pain.

Divesting

Guided by O'Green and a thoroughly reengaged Thornton, Litton eventually got out of the typewriter business altogether, having never found a way to beat or even be competitive with industry leader IBM. Litton sold its dental, X-ray equipment and publishing companies. It reduced its involvement in the machine tool industry and walked away from office equipment and furniture. Also sold were the check imprinting, business labels and special paper companies. Gone or soon to go were Stouffer Foods, a refrigeration equipment business, parts of Litton's aerial survey and revenue control systems operations, a once-promising highway and rapid transit commuter fare collection system, most of its Power Transmission division and several other "small product lines." When the cash register company, Svenska Dataregister, was sold back to Swedish buyers in 1976, it ended Litton's "point-of-sale" ambitions, an idea that was ahead of its time.

Essentially, explained one Litton executive, "If the market didn't look like it was going to grow, if we were not or did not have the potential to become number one or two in the marketplace, we weren't going to be in the business."[26]

Among the factories closed down were Imperial Typewriter in the United Kingdom (2,000 employees), Svenska Dataregister in Sweden (2,500 employees) and machine-tool operations in France (1,000 employees).[27]

In a speech years later, O'Green admitted that the factory closings were tough, but necessary.

"[They were] accomplished at considerable expense in the face of heavy socialistic government influence ... in the United Kingdom, Sweden, France, and Portugal. We were barred from our plants by hostile unions, and we experienced the seizure of company assets by our employees, along with difficulties from the courts, legislative bodies and bureaucrats.... The process was costly and extremely disruptive for many of our loyal employees. It was, however, required to meet our performance targets."[28]

According to its 1973 annual report, Litton showed a profit that fiscal year, with $43 million in net earnings on revenues of over $2.6 billion.[29] However, the next year was a tough one. Revenue climbed above $3 billion, but write-offs involving the struggling business systems and equipment segment totaled $77 million pretax, and losses soared to $40 million,[30] a turnaround of more than $83 million.

While O'Green busily redeployed Litton assets, selling off products and product lines and closing entire divisions, profits returned in 1975 and continued until 1978.

Through the mid- and late-1970s, Litton's top management spent much of its time putting out fires, although it did have flourishing businesses that enabled Litton to spend substantially on much-needed research and development from 1974 to 1979.

As McDaniel recalled, O'Green "immediately began to go out there where the problem was, and he'd sit down with the executives and the engineers and the financial people.... He'd roll up his sleeves, and he'd get to the bottom of whatever problem it was and see to it that it was solved. We had terrible operating problems all over the country and all over the world. In the course of this, we all realized that we were over-conglomerated. We were too diversified. What Fred did at this time was to begin the process of reconceptualizing the company."[31]

New Management Style

Perhaps the outstanding characteristic of the Litton corporate culture at that time was independence — sometimes too much independence — especially at the division level. When it worked,

it worked well, as talented people were given the freedom to use their talents in creative ways, but there was an absence of cohesion, too, a failure to provide guidance and oversight that led to trouble over the long term, especially in an organization as complex as Litton.

No one wanted iron control within the company. The key was to find the right touch. While Ash characterized his style as "just lightly holding the reins on a bunch of thoroughbreds,"[32] O'Green needed to tighten the reins, but not too much. The division presidents retained a high degree of autonomy, but corporate headquarters held a much firmer grip on the reins.

"Corporate involvement in operations is much deeper," O'Green explained. "We have policy guidelines, targets, goals and expectations. We delegate responsibility and authority to the divisions, and we expect them to come forward with plans and to make decisions. If we have good cause to alter a plan or participate more, we do. Tex and I have review responsibility. We listen, ask questions. We don't give much quarter

With O'Green at Litton's helm, group heads met each month for a meeting of "the wise men." Some of the wise men are pictured here, including (left to right) Charles Thornton, chairman of the board; Fred O'Green, president; Joseph S. Imirie, executive vice president and head of the Professional Services and Equipment group; and Ralph H. O'Brien, executive vice president and head of the Business Systems and Equipment group.

for poor performance, but we recognize there are mitigating circumstances where good numbers can't happen."[33]

The heart of the new style could be seen in the monthly operating meeting, in which corporate officers met with the heads and staff officers of Litton's major lines of business, known in Litton parlance as the meeting of "the wise men." The group heads gave forecasts, exchanged sales information and talked about opportunities, profits, return on assets, liquidity, inventory and head counts. In return, corporate officers gave updates on legislation, litigation, money markets, international markets, and political and regulatory activity. A typical meeting ran three hours, and the goal was for everyone to leave with an overview of Litton's world.

O'Green described the meeting as "the toning of the whole operation," with "a single set of numbers for everyone." That was quite a change, even from the recent past, when only a few executives had a broad picture of the company, its opportunities and problems. O'Green also used regional and monthly meetings around the country to spot talented people who could move up.

The "wise men" insisted "that the operating executives tell them everything of consequence that happened in or to the company,"[34] and they traveled constantly for face-to-face meetings with Litton managers all over the world. As one top executive said, "We want no surprises now."[35]

Executive compensation came in for more control too. Simply improving the bottom line in their areas wasn't enough. Executives were rewarded for their returns on gross assets and capital used, plus more subjective standards such as marketplace performance, excellence in planning, and long-range research and development.

Litton's technology also came in for a closer look. In the past, as a result of the fabled Litton independence, one division might be working on something that had already been perfected at another, and rival divisions kept secrets from each other. O'Green's restructuring coordinated technology throughout the company.

The divisions remained independent by normal business standards. As late as 1980, each of the more than 100 divisions did its own planning, with help from corporate.

Explained O'Green, "The ground rules we give them are: assume a constant dollar and exchange rate; don't be an economist, but if there are recognizable cycles in your own business, use them; assume you will stay in the areas you are in now, and if a product fits, buy it; don't start any new business; if you see opportunities, tell us; assume there will be adequate capital for expansion and improved technology. This gives us a forecast that is not pie-in-the-sky, but not too pessimistic."[36]

O'Green promoted international sales by becoming personally involved in the decision to allow divisions outside the United States to develop products for their respective countries. Both LITEF and Litton Italia, for example, became national assets in their respective countries as a result of developing their own avionics products. O'Green actively reviewed the bidding process and acted as referee to resolve internal disputes over product and bidding responsibility in favor of the European operations.

O'Green's involvement in international operations extended far beyond his time at Litton. His far-sightedness rewarded LITEF and Litton Italia sales on the Tornado program of over $900 million by 1999, sales that could not have been won, according to LITEF President Richard Hopman, "without indigenous European technology — Litton technology."[37] And because LITEF and Litton Italia had products of their own, they became major players in the European avionics scene, as illustrated by the success of the Typhoon Eurofighter program, which began in the late 1990s.

Trouble in the Water

Although the Thornton-O'Green management system was informal, the usual division of labor had Thornton handling financial, legal and public relations, while O'Green was immersed in operations. Between them, they had plenty to do. Meanwhile, however, problems had been brewing at the Ingalls shipyard with the Total Package Procurement policy — problems that threatened the very existence of the company.

Total Package Procurement was the brainchild of one of Thornton's old friends from the Whiz Kids, Defense Secretary Robert McNamara. Under the policy, the U.S. Navy delegated to Litton total responsibility for design, construction and fleet readiness, but the Navy had always had control over the design of its ships and wasn't happy about delegating that responsibility to a contractor.

Total Package Procurement attempted to fix at least an approximate price at the beginning of a contract. However, it took several years to build ships, so certain parameters were set and re-estimates of price made at specific stages, with payment set according to stages of completion. However, the Navy required thousands of change orders as the ships were built, just as it always had. These change orders naturally and dramatically increased the expense of shipbuilding.

And there were other problems. Defining cost overruns and cost change orders was common to all shipbuilders, but the Navy and Litton had sharp differences on what were cost overruns (Litton's responsibility) and what were change orders (the Navy's responsibility). Also, because Litton was the only shipbuilder that implemented the highly efficient modular construction, there was some debate over allocation of startup costs.

Additionally, through most of the 1970s manpower and materials were in short supply, deliveries were unpredictable, and inflation was galloping out of control, a particularly acute problem in shipbuilding because it takes several years to build a ship. In congressional testimony,

O'Green offered some examples: Steel plates that once required an 8- to 10-week order lead time now had to be ordered 20 to 24 weeks in advance, and copper cable rose from $1.10 per foot to $1.88 per foot from 1973 to 1974 alone.[38]

While the annual inflation rate approached 20 percent during some years in the 1970s, the Office of Management and Budget limited the Navy to an unrealistic 4.5 percent annual inflation rate to use in its cost projections.

Finally, the shipyard had geared up massively for the Navy contracts. The order for 30 destroyers was the largest such order in the history of the country. As a result, the shipyard employed about 25,000 workers, compared to a norm of 15,000. Even a brief halt in payments was crippling because Ingalls still had to meet its payroll.

The hideously complicated situation resulted in litigation on both sides, and Ingalls wasn't getting paid. The work cost $4 million a week, but there was no hope of repayment until the litigation was concluded, and that appeared to be years away.

At one level it seemed absurd. As John Preston, senior vice president and general counsel, said in a

The Spruance design has been so successful that its basic hull design and powerplant have been used in subsequent cruisers and destroyers.

The Ingalls shipyard delivered 35 ships, nearly two-thirds of all the combatant ships built for the U.S. Navy from 1975 to 1980. They were all built under Total Package Procurement.

1998 interview, "We had the government saying, 'You're responsible for the whole thing,' but at the same time saying, 'I want to tell you how to do it.'"[39]

The situation almost broke Litton Industries.

Ironically, the ships themselves were spectacular. The first, the USS *Spruance,* came off the shipyard in 1975, and Vice Admiral Robert C. Gooding, commander, Naval Sea Systems Command, testified before the Sea Power Subcommittee of the House Armed Services Committee that it was "a destroyerman's dream."[40]

Undoubtedly, there was fault on both sides. An article in *Sea Power* magazine, published by the Navy League of the United States, called Litton "over-optimistic ... in its evaluation of the availability of the skilled labor" at the same time that it underestimated "the startup difficulties ... in getting its assembly line ... yard into full production."[41]

However, the magazine added that most of the fault was elsewhere. The Navy, the Office of Management and Budget, and the Defense Department were "vigorously and justifiably criticized ... for what can only be described as an unrealistic and unprofessional approach to the art and business of shipbuilding."[42]

While Litton was mostly right in its dispute with the Navy, being right didn't get the money flowing again. "We would have meeting after meeting with Navy officials, and it always ended with sweet assurances that we should go ahead and build the ships and they would see us in court," recalled McDaniel. "In other words, we might get some money after 10 years of grueling litigation."[43]

This was "a great crisis in the life of Charles B. Thornton," added McDaniel. "He couldn't believe that anybody was treating his Litton Industries the way they were. Thornton was, for the first time in his life, ineffective as a negotiator."[44]

In desperation, the Litton legal team came up with a bold plan: Stop work on the ships in defiance of the contract and sue the Navy for $1 billion.

It was risky, to say the least. The contract stipulated that if the contractor was in default, the Navy could move the ships to another shipyard, finish them there and charge Litton the difference in cost, which certainly would have put Litton in bankruptcy.

But Litton's lawyers believed that the Navy would do no such thing simply because it was not in the Navy's best interest. The Navy's best interest was to get the ships.

In a 1997 speech, McDaniel described the tense atmosphere: "I will never forget the day that [Litton senior vice president] Bob Lentz and I walked into Fred O'Green's office and asked him to do something that no businessman would ever dream of doing — refuse to perform a contract with your best customer and sue that customer for $1 billion. It was unthinkable. I suspect that Fred's arm shriveled a little bit that day, but he signed the letter."[45] Ingalls stopped work on August 1, 1976.

As expected, the Justice Department filed suit in federal court in Jackson, Mississippi, asking for an injunction compelling Litton to continue building. When the arguments were completed, Judge Harold Cox ruled in Litton's favor. Said Cox: "The United States has entered this Court seeking equity. It is in the same position, no better and no worse, than the humblest litigant. The principles of equity require that in order to obtain equity you must do equity. Therefore, I will issue an order requiring the defendant to continue to build the ships, but only on the condition that the government pay to the contractor 92 percent of his costs every week."[46]

"That statement saved Litton Industries," declared McDaniel.[47]

Settlement

With the logjam broken, both sides began negotiations to settle the mess. In June 1978, Litton finally negotiated a settlement of $460 million on the ships. The settlement required two acts of Congress, one to agree and the other to appropriate the money. At the same time, Litton agreed to absorb a pre-tax loss of $332,573,000, which it did in 1978.

Predictably, those negotiations were as difficult as any other part of this grueling marathon. O'Green, McDaniel and Litton controller Wayne Grosvenor bounced back and forth between Los Angeles and Washington, D.C., for months trying to bring an end to the long nightmare.

"We were all under an enormous strain," McDaniel said. "On one of those occasions, on the way back in the company plane, I fainted dead away."[48]

Still, now that the crippling problem was out of the way, if anyone else at Litton fainted, it was probably from relief. The medicine was bitter — Litton's almost $333 million pre-tax write-off in 1978 resulted in a $91 million loss that year — but it did bring a cure. The following year, Litton's earnings were $189 million, a $280 million turnaround.

As a side note, the policy of Total Package Procurement wasn't used often and never worked when it did. Out of a half-dozen such contracts, Litton had two, for the LHAs

The Landing Helicopter Assault (LHA) ships were built under the U.S. Navy's new Total Package Procurement contract, an approach that turned out to be quite damaging to both Litton and the Navy.

and the Spruance-class destroyers. The rest were divided among other defense contractors, and each resulted in heavy losses for the contractor. Although Total Package Procurement was in place before he took office in 1976, President Jimmy Carter eventually issued a statement to the effect that it was a mistake and an unfair method of contracting.

The Phoenix Rises

A company's spectacular rise and fall was not unusual in the transition from the 1960s to the economically calamitous 1970s. As one reporter noted, Litton was unusual because it was able to rise again. After a hard-earned makeover, Litton Industries was a revitalized company.[49]

The news was good and getting better. Litton set a new sales record of $3.7 billion in fiscal year 1978. By the end of 1979, Litton was whittled down to 76,000 employees. The re-tooled Litton was based on high technology and the direction of that technology toward the creation of new products and the modernization of older, familiar products.

Overall, electronic components were fast becoming a major profit-maker for Litton — a change from the company's past reliance on defense and business systems. This was partially due to Litton's increased emphasis on commercial products and partially due to the admirable leadership of Arnold Kaufman. According to Donald Lepore, who later became group executive for Litton's highly successful Electronic Components and Materials group, Kaufman was largely responsible for the success of

Electronic Components and Materials throughout the 1970s and early 1980s. Through his keen insight into people and business, Kaufman was able to pull together a large cross section of businesses — many of which seemed hopeless when they were acquired — allowing them to grow internally and turning them into profitable enterprises.[50]

In 1979 and 1980, Litton's comeback was cemented by a series of large contracts, including a $1.64 billion contract with Saudi Arabia for a nationwide air-defense system, incorporating radar, computers and communications. Though Litton had to sign a fixed-price contract, Saudi Arabia gave a substantial prepayment, which served as a safeguard against loss through inflation. In addition, Litton was building an air-traffic control system for each of Saudi Arabia's major airports. Litton also landed a $1 billion–plus contract to provide inertial navigation systems for all U.S. cruise missiles.[51]

With oil and gas exploration at record levels around the world, Western Geophysical, possessor of the largest data bank of worldwide geological formations, was a gold mine. With sales of $300 million in 1979, its clients included major oil companies, independents and national companies such as PEMEX in Mexico and Brazil's Petrobras. Western Geophysical had computer centers in London, Singapore, Milan and Calgary, plus a new plant in Alvin, Texas, that assembled vibrator and recording trucks. The complex vehicles were used for seismic work from jungle to desert. In addition, its fleet of 30 seismic vessels explored the world's oceans and seas.[52]

Western Geophysical vibrator trucks send sound waves into the earth in search of oil.

Litton also had thriving new businesses in passive detection systems (computerized listening devices that locate radar), as well as tactical command and control, and communications systems.

And of course, Litton was still the leader in aircraft inertial navigation in both the military and commercial markets, enjoying a robust 60 percent share of the latter. In 1975, Litton's Aero Products added 15 new commercial airlines as customers for its inertial systems, bringing the total to 55 worldwide.

By 1980, Aero Products' commercial ring laser gyro inertial reference system was standard navigation equipment for some of the new wide-body jetliners. This system employed three laser gyroscopes and significantly improved navigational performance compared to previous technology while reducing both size and weight. The laser gyro system was perfectly suited for the computerized cockpits of the "new generation" aircraft, which were equipped with digital instrumentation.[53]

A Fallen Leader

Although Litton's commercial and industry businesses remained weak, no one could deny that Litton Industries had experienced a major comeback. Then life began to overshadow business. Tex Thornton was dying.

It began with discomfort in Thornton's left shoulder sometime in the spring of 1981. Later tests confirmed that Thornton had cancer. After the diagnosis, Thornton agreed to make O'Green chief executive officer, in addition to O'Green's other duties, but he resolved to remain chairman himself. A worn-out Thornton presided over his last board meeting on September 1, 1981. Thornton asked that his son, Charles B. Thornton, Jr., be named to the board. O'Green became CEO on October 1.

On September 3, Thornton received a call from Michael Deaver, President Ronald Reagan's chief assistant. Thornton was to receive the Medal of Freedom, the nation's highest civilian honor, and he was invited to the White House for the ceremony.

As much as Thornton wanted to go, he was too ill to make the trip. His wife, Flora, and their two sons, Charles, Jr. and Laney, went in his place for the October 9 ceremony.

Litton founder Charles Bates "Tex" Thornton died on November 24, 1981.

Before the family accepted the award, President Reagan read the citation:

"To Charles B. 'Tex' Thornton, industrialist, warrior and humanitarian. Tex Thornton's life has embodied all that is best in the worlds of commerce, military service and civic duty. In all three realms, he has never failed to give generously of his boundless energy, his unfailing courage and his deep love of country. In war and peace, in the public service and the private sector, Tex Thornton has earned the esteem of all Americans who value patriotism, enterprise and compassion as cornerstones of our nation's greatness."

The ceremony was taped so that Thornton could watch it at home, where his condition deteriorated swiftly. He fell into a coma on November 23 and died just before midnight on November 24, 1981.

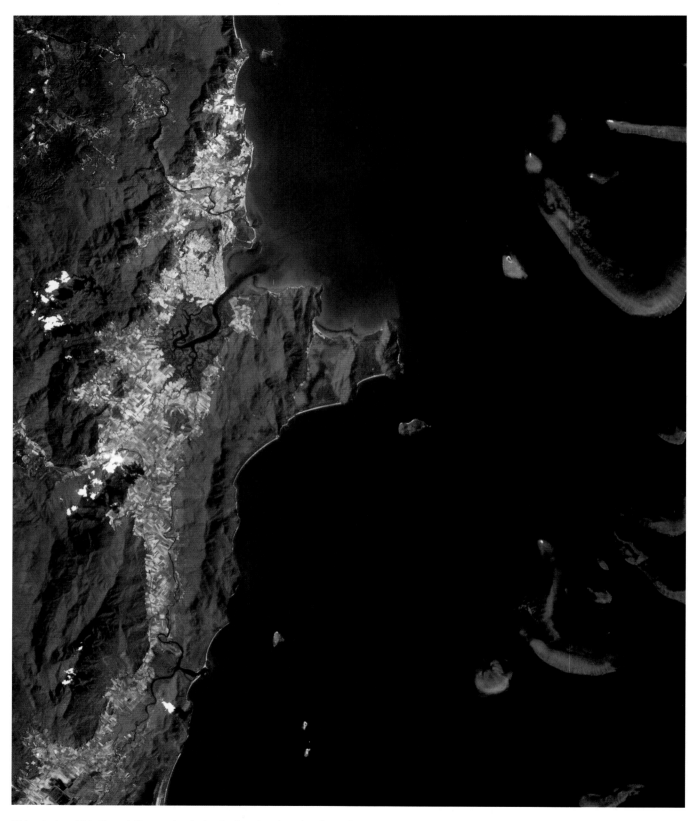

This photo of Northeast Queensland, Australia, showing the Great Barrier Reef, was shot by a Large Format Camera designed and manufactured by Litton's Itek Optical Systems division for NASA.

CHAPTER SEVEN

STAYING ON TOP
1982–1988

*"We continue to commit our resources to internal research and devel-
opment and acquisition programs in order to achieve our goal: to be a preeminent supplier of high technology products and services in each of our
business areas."*

— Fred O'Green and Orion Hoch, 1984[1]

T HE ASCENDANCE OF RONALD Reagan to the presidency in 1980 heralded enormous changes in the United States, including less govern- mental control in the marketplace, increased consumer spending and lim- itations on organized labor. On the international front, Reagan battled communism throughout the world by providing massive American military and economic support to anti-Marxist forces, spurring a heavy increase in defense spending. The United States embarked on a huge arms buildup in both conventional and nuclear forces. Besides Reagan's announcement to build a 600-ship navy, he initiated the much-publicized Strategic Defense Initiative (SDI or "Star Wars") missile defense program.

This trend continued until 1987, when Soviet Premier Mikhail Gorbachev and Reagan agreed to eliminate intermediate-range nuclear weapons — the first step toward ending the arms race.[2]

Litton was in a prime position to support the military buildup, and the company wasn't slow to seize the opportunity. Like much of the American economy in the mid-eighties, Litton's business flourished, giving the company ample opportunity to grow, not only through acquisi- tion, but also through what it did best — techno- logical development.

By the mid-1980s, Litton Industries was nearing the end of its efforts to refocus the company and concen- trate on three core business areas: defense, industrial automation and resource exploration.[3] These were astute selections considering that, by that time, electronics accounted for over one-third of the total cost of many U.S. defense systems and that Litton was a leader in most areas of defense electronics.[4]

The technical requirements, capabilities and possibilities in these fields would have seemed almost impossible a few years earlier. They cer- tainly were unforeseen when Charles Litton sold his small Northern California electronics company in 1953. But what once seemed like science fiction had become matter-of-fact and routine in a very short time for Litton Industries. Although Litton was only 30 years old in 1983, the technology on which it based most of its business had under- gone remarkable changes.

A next-generation land warrior demonstrates a Litton-produced Handheld Terminal Unit integral to the ongoing U.S. Army program to standardize and maximize the digitization of air defense, combat service support, field artillery, intelligence and electronic warfare, and maneuver control.

Evolution of a System

In a significant milestone in aviation history, on August 26, 1983, Air France received Aero Products' 20,000th inertial navigation system for the airline's new Airbus A310-200.[5] Air France was Aero Products' first international customer for an inertial navigation system when it equipped its Boeing 707 in 1967. Then, in 1969, Air France became the first international carrier to use inertial systems as the sole means of navigation over the North Atlantic.

By 1983, Aero Products was in its third generation of inertial navigation technology with the LTN-90-100 and LTN-92, and Litton systems flew

with 80 airlines, as well as operating within military aircraft, land vehicles, missiles, ships and torpedoes. "It was a milestone discovery when we recognized our inertial guidance technology was not just confined to aircraft," said Joseph Caligiuri, retired executive vice president who headed Litton's Advanced Electronic Systems group. "With a little redesign and so forth, we could apply it to everything that needed to know where it was located, direction of vertical, attitude, heading, position or velocity information."[6]

Litton's engineering had come a long way. The first inertial system, developed at the Massachusetts Institute of Technology, weighed more than 2,500 pounds, compared to only 44 pounds for the LTN-90-100.

Aero Products' first-generation commercial systems in the 1960s, the LTN-51 and LTN-58, were gear-driven analog devices equipped with a series of complex and cumbersome electro-mechanical devices. Despite the bulky mechanism, the LTN-51 and LTN-58 were so hardy and reliable that an estimated 1,700 of them were still flying in 1983.[7]

Aero Products' second generation commercial systems, the LTN-72 and the LTN-72R, used vibragimbal gyros with upgraded electronics and more powerful computers.[8]

The division's third generation commercial systems, the LTN-90-100 and the LTN-92, which replaced the early LTN-58 and LTN-51 inertial systems, featured the laser gyro as the heart of the system. A laser spun counter-rotating light beams around a small optical circuit to sense and measure changes in motion. The system was then developed as a gyroscope to help guide ships, aircraft, missiles and space vehicles.[9]

Three-ring laser gyros, three accelerometers and associated electronics made the LTN-90-100 and LTN-92 remarkably accurate and reliable systems. "The ring laser changed the way we could configure our navigation systems," said Caligiuri.[10] The ability to "strap down" an inertial system directly to the frame of an aircraft or

The Litton inertial navigation system employing ring laser gyro technology is checked out in the cockpit of an Air France A310.

Combined with advanced microprocessor technology, the ring laser gyro inertial reference system, supplied by Litton's Aero Products division, provides critical information for both navigation and flight control.

missile instead of suspending it in a series of complex mechanical gimbals reduced space requirements, made the system much more rigid, simplified navigation tasks and greatly reduced the cost. The strap-down concept also reduced production and maintenance costs by eliminating rotating parts. There was no friction because there were no moving parts.

Especially considering that it was Aero Products' signature product, delivery of the 20,000th inertial navigation system in 1983 was something to celebrate. As Caligiuri said, "Over the years, Litton's INS systems have gotten smaller in size, more reliable, more accurate and more maintainable. Yet, costs in current dollars have kept level at about $100,000 to $125,000 for the LTN-90-100/LTN-92, which is about the same in then-year dollars of 20 years ago."[11]

Electronic Warfare

Inertial navigation was only one area in which there were extraordinary technological strides. At the time, it was a common complaint that the sheer speed of the technological advances was intimidating. As Litton noted in its 1983 annual report, "Technology compression — the phenomenon that technical advances and breakthroughs occur so rapidly that new programs are obsolete almost before they are employed — places ever mounting challenges before scientists and engineers."[12]

Litton, however, was able to evolve from one technology to another "without missing a beat," in the words of Caligiuri.[13] Consider electronic warfare, which Litton defined as "the art and science of being able to 'see,' identify and render harmless a wide variety of hostile electronic threats, ranging from radar-equipped enemy aircraft to surface-to-air missile batteries, and even spy satellites."[14]

As often happens during war, necessity became the mother of invention. During the Vietnam War, U.S. fighter and support aircraft had trouble avoiding enemy surface-to-air missiles (SAMs). Litton's Applied Technology Division (ATD), formerly Itek before Litton acquired it, launched a crash program to find a way to warn pilots that their aircraft had been "seen" by enemy SAMs and/or anti-aircraft artillery radar so that the pilots could take evasive action or employ countermeasures to confuse and mislead the enemy.

With the country in the midst of a controversial war and casualties mounting, the ATD engineers were faced with the challenge of developing this new technology very quickly. They did it within 90 days, which paved the way for Litton to eventually become "the unchallenged leader in threat warning," including "particular competence in systems for surveillance, detection and analysis of enemy radar 'signatures,' optical and laser imaging and threat warning for aircraft."[15]

In 1979, Litton Data Systems embarked on a program to put its highly sophisticated command, control, communications and intelligence (C^3I) technology — originally developed to defend against air attack in the 1950s and 1960s —

into the hands of the battlefield soldier. It took until well into the 1980s before the goal was achieved. The system gathered and provided information to commanders and front-line troops as the events were happening. The heart of the system was a portable, battery-powered, briefcase-sized terminal that weighed 35 pounds. The terminal was linked to high-speed digital radio communications with forward observers equipped with hand-held terminals that weighed less than five pounds. The information was displayed both graphically and alpha-numerically. A variety of software programs allowed the system to target artillery and mortar barrages, put together short-range air defense, assess personnel strength and compile battlefield logistics.[16]

Litton's onboard threat warning system detects when an enemy surface-to-air missile radar is tracking the aircraft and warns the pilot through a cockpit display to take evasive action or employ countermeasures.

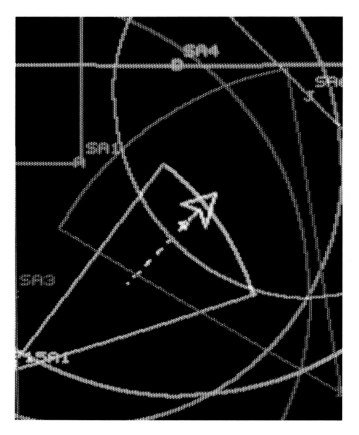

In 1986, the Data Systems division also began delivery of its newest C³I system, the AN/TYQ-23 Tactical Air Operations Central/Modular Control Equipment (TAOC/MCE), to the U.S. Marines and Air Force. These 20-foot modules contained computers, operator consoles and voice and digital data link communications equipment for battlefield air surveillance and control.[17]

Over sixty computers were embedded in the new modules. The combination of computing power and advanced packaging meant that new capabilities could be provided in a package light enough to be transported to the battlefield by a standard Marine Corps helicopter. The system was an enormous improvement in size, weight and capacity over the previous generation Litton had developed for the Marine Corps in the early 1960s.[18]

Since the 1970s, Litton's Electron Tube Division (ETD) had been producing high-resolution cathode ray tubes for military and civilian use. This optical technology spun off into microchannel plate image intensifier tubes, which became the heart of night vision goggles.[19] ETD provided the majority of the U.S. Army's PVS-5A night vision devices, including 3,000 night vision units in 1981 alone.[20] Litton was also a major supplier of night vision scopes to law enforcement agencies across the country.[21] Later, the night vision business became a part of the Electro-Optical Systems division.

ETD's other new developments included the world's first production, dual-mode coupled cavity tube used in the F-16 radar system, plus traveling wave tubes (TWTs) for the airborne self-protection jammer system. In addition, ETD was the only company to develop a stretched-band M-BWO (m-type backward wave oscillator) for the B-52, and its advanced medium-range, air-to-air missile TWT had proprietary technical features, which put the division in a class by itself.[22]

Acquired by Litton in 1983, International Laser Systems, later renamed Laser Systems, created the first laser radar used in space as part of the U.S. Department of Defense's Strategic Defense Initiative (Star Wars). "Our company won the contract prior to Litton acquiring us, and we were executing it during the period shortly after the acquisition by Litton," said Robert Del Boca, president of Laser Systems. "To create this, we looked at the characteristics of reentry vehicles and various other

Litton's night vision goggles intensify images for military and law enforcement personnel.

Far right: A Western Geophysical seismic survey ship sails through Alaskan waters.

Below: Ingalls modernized the World War II battleship USS *Iowa* so that it could be redeployed with the fleet. The *Iowa* hadn't been to sea since the 1950s.

characteristics to see if identification of the targets could be accomplished."[23]

Success at Ingalls

Shipbuilding was another area that benefited enormously from technology's rapid march. Until the 20th century, the basic outlines of shipbuilding had not changed for thousands of years. In the 1960s, Litton introduced modern shipbuilding techniques to the United States with its modular construction site at the Ingalls shipyard in Pascagoula, Mississippi.

"At first, there was some skepticism about modular construction," explained Ingalls Vice President Dave Wright, "but when we started producing the destroyers, launching them at one a month and delivering one every six weeks, it became pretty obvious to everybody that this was a pretty good way to go."[24]

Once the bugs of modular construction were worked out and the shipyard resolved its monumental contractual problems with the U.S. government, the modular program was a stunning success. From 1975 to 1983, Ingalls designed, built and delivered to the U.S. Navy no less than 41 surface combat ships — more than all the other domestic shipyards combined.[25]

One of many reasons for Ingalls' speed and efficiency was that Litton had introduced a computerized design and manufacturing system intended to streamline and automate the process of ship-building, especially the complex warships at which Ingalls excelled.

Naval architects and engineers applied the specifications of a ship's design to a computer-based interactive graphics system. The design became the master data base and was used for quality assurance, manufacturing planning, inventory ordering and control, and production operations. The design changes and updates were instantly available, and all the information every step of the way was derived directly from this base, which ensured increased speed and enhanced precision.[26]

"Using our computer program for ship design gives us significant advantages," explained Den Knecht, vice president for public and industrial relations at Ingalls. "With the old way of designing the ship, a draftsman worked on a drawing board, but you're limited with that because you can operate only in two dimensions. On the drawing, you may not be able to see that there's an interference if you're running, for example, an air conditioning duct and a pipe, but the computer system does the interference tracking for you while you're still in the drawing stage."[27]

Two of the largest shipyard contracts in the 1980s involved the Ticonderoga-class cruiser and the LHD amphibious assault ship programs.

The USS *Ticonderoga* was the first ship with the Aegis weapons system, the most advanced air defense, radar and missile system in the world. Named for the shield of the Greek and Roman gods, it was described as "the eyes, ears and fist of a Navy task force."[28] The guided-missile cruiser gave the U.S. fleet greatly improved defense against missiles, aircraft and submarines.

The Aegis weapons system was the primary protection for the Navy's aircraft carrier battle groups. Designed to work in "extreme threat environments," the cruisers could detect, classify and track hundreds of potential targets simultaneously in the air, on the surface and under the sea and quickly orchestrate a response to such saturation attacks. Its weaponry included torpedoes and antisubmarine rockets, deck guns, surface-to-surface and surface-to-air missiles, rapid fire close-in weapons, and electronic jammers and decoys. Despite its impressive capabilities, the *Ticonderoga* operated with a crew of only 360, compared to a minimum of 800-plus that were needed to operate World War II cruisers.[29]

Ingalls' work on the Aegis cruisers was rated as "outstanding" by the U.S. Navy, a rating that helped ensure future contracts.[30]

Another shipbuilding program important to Ingalls at this time involved the LHDs, a new class of amphibious assault ships, which were a modified version of the earlier LHAs. These 40,500-ton, general purpose amphibious assault ships cost about $1 billion each and were designed to deploy and land a force of 2,000 U.S. Marines, supported by Harrier jet aircraft and helicopters. They also contained full hospitals with several operating rooms.

Also, in 1983 Ingalls won contracts to overhaul the USS *Iowa* and the USS *Wisconsin*, two of the four famous Iowa-class battleships completed during World War II, which had been in mothballs since the 1950s.[31] This conversion was the brainchild of Chief Naval Officer Tom Hayward, who viewed the ships as floating platforms capable of launching a very large number of cruise missiles. After he retired from the Navy, Hayward joined Litton's board of directors.[32]

Exploring the Depths

In seismic exploration, the domain of another successful Litton division, the progress wasn't in speed (although gaining access to information was much enhanced compared to just a few years earlier) but in the depth, quality and accuracy of information.

Prior to Litton's innovation, seismic explorers measured the earth's vibrations using a cumbersome apparatus cranked by hand to make traces of squiggly lines across photographic paper. This camera-like device contained "harp" wires vibrated by vacuum-tube amplifiers transmitting seismic signals.

By the 1980s, Western Geophysical, Litton's seismic exploration division, was performing the same procedure using digital computers, a practice that was pioneered by Texas Instruments.[33] Digital data acquisition was able to record and process 10 billion to 20 billion samples of information from a single 10-square-mile survey area.[34] The computer then refined the image to convert it to a graphic, realistic image of the earth's sub-surface.

This 3-D isometric map, used by Litton's Resource Exploration Services, shows a petroleum reservoir thousands of feet underground.

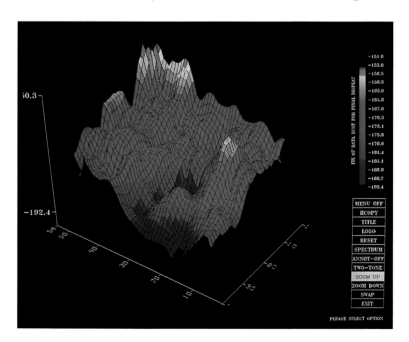

With three-dimensional color video imaging, another new tool, a computer terminal displayed what resembled a cube sliced from beneath the earth, one that could be pulled out and examined from every angle by computer. The increased coverage and density created graphics that were 10 times more detailed and accurate than anything that had come before.[35] Experts not only had the information, they could now see how it looked.

One of the primary purposes of seismic exploration is to find the most suitable places to drill for oil and natural gas, with clients buying the service based on the accuracy of information. But much of the world's oil and gas is underwater, and drilling underwater presents its own array of problems.

In fact, until the 1920s, such drilling simply wasn't done. The first underwater well struck oil only a few feet from shore in Venezuela's Lake Maracaibo in 1928.[36] By the 1980s, an oil platform in the Gulf of Mexico was producing oil in 1,025 feet of water, and drilling ships had operated in more than 5,600 feet of water in the Mediterranean Sea.[37]

But the risk of drilling underwater was too high without a comprehensive survey of what lay beneath the ocean floor, and Litton's LRS-16 Kiloseis system was far and away the leader in that field. To gather information several miles beneath the ocean floor, a two-mile "streamer" cable packed with several thousand hydrophone sensors was towed 30 to 40 feet below the water's surface behind a seismic survey ship. Every 10 seconds, air "guns" generated acoustic pulses at frequencies that were low enough to penetrate the ocean floor. As the acoustic waves traveled several miles deep into the earth, the various strata reflected a portion of that acoustic energy up to the sensors in the cable, which returned the information to sensors on the ship, storing billions of bits of information in high-density magnetic tape.[38] The information was then processed into easily readable form by sophisticated on-shore computers.

In 1987, Litton created a new subsidiary, Western Atlas International, which combined Litton's Resources Exploration group and the Atlas division of Dresser Industries. The union resulted in a "new Litton subsidiary with a broader capacity

A Litton Industrial Automation automated monorail system transports cars at a General Motors plant in Canada.

for serving the energy industry."[39] Litton and Dresser each received 50 percent of the common stock of Western Atlas.[40]

The new Houston-based company combined Litton capabilities in seismic exploration, reservoir description, data reduction and interpretation with Dresser Atlas' expertise in wireline oil well logging, which involved getting sophisticated instruments down into the bore hole of an oil well to obtain detailed information about the geographical strata.

American Industry

The same technological prowess used in fighter aircraft and seismic exploration could be effectively applied in other endeavors as well. By the 1980s, there was a great deal of conjecture about the factory of the future and how it might evolve, perhaps even in an environment without human workers. Whatever the future held, Litton strove to position itself on the cutting edge of industrial automation, especially in the area of moving and handling everything from raw material to finished goods.

A breakthrough by Litton's Unit Handling Systems division integrated material handling

systems into the manufacturing process with automated material handling and storage and retrieval systems. These systems were adaptable to a variety of circumstances, ranging from gigantic foundries to meticulously detailed operations for the newest electronic products.[41]

It took about 170 years from the onset of the Industrial Revolution before numerically controlled machines that received instructions from a code punched into paper tape were in common use. Within 20 years after that, factories had begun using machines that were linked with electronic systems and had automatic transfer lines that could move a part through several steps performed by a number of different machines.[42]

Litton's Landis Tool division developed a state-of-the-art machine computer control system specifically designed for manufacturing flexibility. Instead of having several machines perform different operations, the same machine could perform various operations on a variety of parts.

COMPLETING THE COMEBACK

ALTHOUGH LITTON'S RESTRUCTURING would continue for some time and was always thought to be a "work in progress," by the early 1980s Litton Industries was nearing the end of its major effort to "sharpen the focus" of the company.[1]

After what the *Economist* called Litton's "long convalescence from its tumble in the early 1970s, followed by its costly wrangle with the Pentagon over defence contracts," Litton was once again, the publication noted, "on the prowl."[2]

Litton had accumulated as much as $1.5 billion in cash because it had stopped gobbling up other companies and had taken to hoarding cash instead. When falling interest rates made cash less attractive — in 1983, declining interest rates alone lowered Litton's income by $30 million[3] — the company started buying.

Chief among these acquisitions was Itek, for which it paid $240 million in 1983, its first big acquisition in years. Itek manufactured products based on optical and electronic technology for the aerial reconnaissance and surveillance, defense electronics, and graphics markets and was Litton's first big acquisition in the electronic warfare business.[4]

Another significant acquisition was International Laser Systems, purchased for $45 million, which produced laser systems for scientific, experimental and defense applications.

All in all, Litton increased its realm of expertise in Advanced Electronics and Defense with several important acquisitions:
- Instrument & Life Support (aircraft oxygen supply and generation) in March 1982
- Itek, in February 1983
- International Laser Systems in May 1983
- Pietzsch (land vehicle stabilization systems) in April 1984
- Parks-Jaggers Aerospace (fire control and electric optical systems) in June 1984

In Geophysical Exploration & Services, Litton acquired several key companies:
- J.S. Nolen (reservoir analysis and simulation software) in November 1983
- Core Laboratories (earth core analysis) in January 1984
- Macrometrics (geodetic survey research) in March 1984
- Downhole Seismic Services (profiling and velocity services) in July 1984
- Petrophysical Service (drilling core measurement and analysis) in August 1984

Litton also acquired companies for its Industrial Automation Systems:
- Taylor Manufacturing (high-speed conveyor systems) in March 1983
- Automated Systems (robot vehicles for material handling) in March 1983
- CITCO (cutting and dressing tools) in August 1983
- Tramex (overhead crane systems) in February 1984
- Gildemeister (computerized flexible manufacturing systems) in August 1984

In the meantime, Litton continued to sell companies that either weren't doing well or had nothing to do with its core businesses. The annual revenue of the companies sold during 1982, 1983 and 1984 totaled almost $800 million.

The company's entire Business Systems segment was sold piecemeal. First, Litton sold the specialty paper, printing and forms business in July 1983. Then it divested business furnishings, which included furniture, office products and store fixtures, in May 1984. Finally, it sold Monroe Systems for Business, manufacturers of office machinery, in October 1984.

All told, the early- to mid-eighties was Litton's most active acquisition and divestiture period since the 1960s, a sign that the company had indeed completed its comeback.

Maintenance was simplified by a display that identified a malfunctioning part by name, part number and location.

Landis' new "machine controller" could be used in the manufacture of products ranging from aircraft to automobiles, which had become an increasingly important, and increasingly large, segment of the market.[43] By the late 1980s, the North American automotive industry was the "largest marketplace" for Litton's Industrial Automation Systems.[44]

Airtron, meanwhile, had branched into gallium arsenide, which would later become one of the division's key products. Recent discoveries had found that gallium arsenide would become a viable commercial material in making high-frequency amplifier chips.[45]

A Sharper Focus

While Litton greatly benefited from the Reagan administration's increased defense spending during the 1980s, the economy in the early years of the decade was "capricious," to use a Litton description, suffering from high interest rates and soft markets at home and abroad.[46]

American manufacturers also faced fierce competition from foreign suppliers. Litton was not the only American company to complain that foreign competitors, notably Japanese, were aided by governments in ways that made competition difficult. Litton eventually was forced to give up on its popular line of microwave ovens, for example, when its prices were badly undercut by Asian-made models. The popular phrase "Japan, Inc." captured the feeling of the time.

As it divested itself of companies that didn't fit, Litton grew cash rich. With as much as $1.5 billion in cash in fiscal 1983, Litton was earning more than $30 million a year in interest alone.[47] In response, Litton became acquisitive again. It was, as one magazine reported, "on the prowl."[48] (See sidebar, page 86.)

In the first years of the decade, however, in response to the shaky economy, Litton had tightened controls and reduced redundancy in operations even further.[49] In 1981, for instance, Litton had 77,000 employees.[50] By 1988, despite a flurry of acquisition throughout the decade, the number of employees had fallen to 55,000.[51]

Several years later, O'Green noted that "corporate restructuring" was not a term used at the time, and it was only "later on that we learned what we had done."[52]

This "refocus" or "restructuring" differed from what Litton did in the early and mid-1970s. At that time, Litton was perceived by many in the business and investment community as being out of control. What was needed then was operational and management discipline.

The restructuring of the 1980s brought Litton into sharper focus for investors and raised shareholder values to levels that were consistent with Litton's capabilities. O'Green said Litton management knew the company was complex in its diversity:

"We were difficult for the investment community to analyze and difficult and time consuming for them to follow. We knew that we were clearly undervalued in the marketplace. The price-earnings multiple on our stock was at 6 ½ at the end of the successful 1982 financial year... [a level that] was hardly appropriate for a company in which over 65 percent of sales was in high-tech electronics where one would expect a multiple more in the range of 12 or higher. The challenge then was to develop our long-term strategy and near-term action plan for raising shareholder values to levels consistent with our performance and true value.

"We also knew that among our high-multiple businesses were a number of low-multiple businesses. This tended to lower our overall market value and made efficient asset allocation difficult. Therefore we concluded we would go forward, reducing Litton to three core businesses [and] ... sell the inherently low-multiple businesses that could not contribute to our long-range rate-of-return objectives."[53]

Rise of a Leader

O'Green didn't do it alone, of course. Just as he was Thornton's right arm for many years, so O'Green had one of his own, a cool and analytical engineer named Orion L. "Orie" Hoch.

When he joined Litton on June 3, 1982, as president and chief operating officer, Hoch already had been one of the famed "LIDOs," or Litton

Industries Dropouts who had left Litton years before to achieve success elsewhere.

Born in Canonsburg, Pennsylvania, in 1928, Hoch graduated from Carnegie-Mellon University in 1952 with a bachelor of science degree in physics. From 1952–1953, he worked at Hughes Aircraft, which was then headed by Tex Thornton. In 1954, he earned a master's degree in physics from UCLA and went on to earn a doctorate in electrical engineering from Stanford University in 1957.

Hoch joined Litton in the company's Electron Devices division the year he graduated from Stanford. Within 11 years he became the division's president and general manager. After two years as vice president of the Components group, Hoch was named a corporate vice president with responsibility for investor and public affairs and then was promoted to senior vice president and deputy head of the Business Systems and Equipment group.

In the way of the LIDOs, Hoch left Litton in 1974 to become president of Advanced Memory Systems in Silicon Valley. When Advanced Memory merged with Intersil, Inc., in 1976, he continued as president of the company. In 1982, after General Electric bought Intersil, he rejoined Litton, even though the acquisition made Hoch a multimillionaire.[54]

Introspective, precise and incisive, Hoch largely ignored the limelight. Even later when he succeeded O'Green at the top of the company, he was rarely quoted and, in contrast to his gregarious predecessors, was rarely the subject of lengthy magazine articles.

Protecting Its Assets

Litton executives give Hoch a great deal of the credit for the company's successful refocus during the eighties. "When Orie Hoch succeeded Fred O'Green, Litton went through a change in its philosophy," said George Fenimore. "At one time, we had as many as 500 subsidiary companies because each of our companies had its own chain of subsidiaries. Orie's philosophy was 'let's not acquire, but let us dispose,' and consequently, Litton got out of a lot of businesses."[55] By 1985, Litton could proudly declare that "our strategic restructuring program was essentially completed."[56]

After O'Green's retirement, Orion L. Hoch (seated) was elected chairman of the board, while Roland O. Peterson (standing) was appointed president and COO.

The stock market obviously considered the program a success as well. A 1984 *Wall Street Journal* story noted that "the price of Litton Industries shares has been rising without fanfare" and had jumped 17 percent, to 67 $\frac{5}{8}$, in only a month.[57]

"Litton no longer is a conglomerate; it's a well-managed, successful high-tech company," said Howard Rubel, an analyst with Cyrus J. Lawrence, Inc.[58]

In the same article, another analyst noted that as a result of its cash-rich position, Litton was "a logical takeover candidate,"[59] a genuine risk in an era when hostile takeovers had reached a peak.

Litton was even more attractive a year later. Fiscal year 1984 was a good one, with Litton earning $313.4 million on sales of $4.6 billion and its stock selling in the mid-70s.[60]

Then on May 24, 1985, Litton announced an ambitious program to buy back $1.3 billion worth of its own common stock and eliminate its dividend. Wall Street liked what it saw. In the week following the announcement, Litton's stock jumped from 77 to 86 ½.

An unidentified investment banker was quoted as marveling at this success. "A couple of years ago, if you had told me a company would sell half its business and the stock would go up, I would have thought you were crazy. But Litton does that, and now it eliminates the dividend, and the stock goes up even more."[61]

The stock buyback program was expanded in 1987. By the end of the 1988 fiscal year, Litton had repurchased 2.6 million shares of its common stock.[62]

Distinguished Service

On March 31, 1988, it came time for Fred O'Green to step down as chairman of the board after 26 years with Litton Industries (although he contin-ued on the board of directors and as chairman of the Executive Committee). O'Green left Litton in excellent shape. Net earnings for the 1988 fiscal year increased 21 percent to $167 million, and sales rose 10 percent to $4.86 billion.[63] Litton was ranked first in the world for inertial navigation systems and was a world leader in both tactical radar warning systems and tactical C^3I systems. The company's Industrial Automation division led the North American market for high-volume integrated manufacturing systems that produced car engines, and the Ingalls shipyard was the number one producer of surface combat ships in the United States.[64]

O'Green had stayed on at least two years longer than the usual retirement age. Hoch, already chief executive officer, now became chairman of the company's board of directors. Roland O. Peterson was named president and chief operating officer, while Joseph T. Casey was named vice chairman and chief financial officer.

In a speech not long after his retirement, O'Green summed up his experience with Litton Industries, which he had helped so much to enhance and rebuild. "All in all, Litton is healthy, exciting and a great place to work," he said. "I have enjoyed every one of my 26 years with the company."

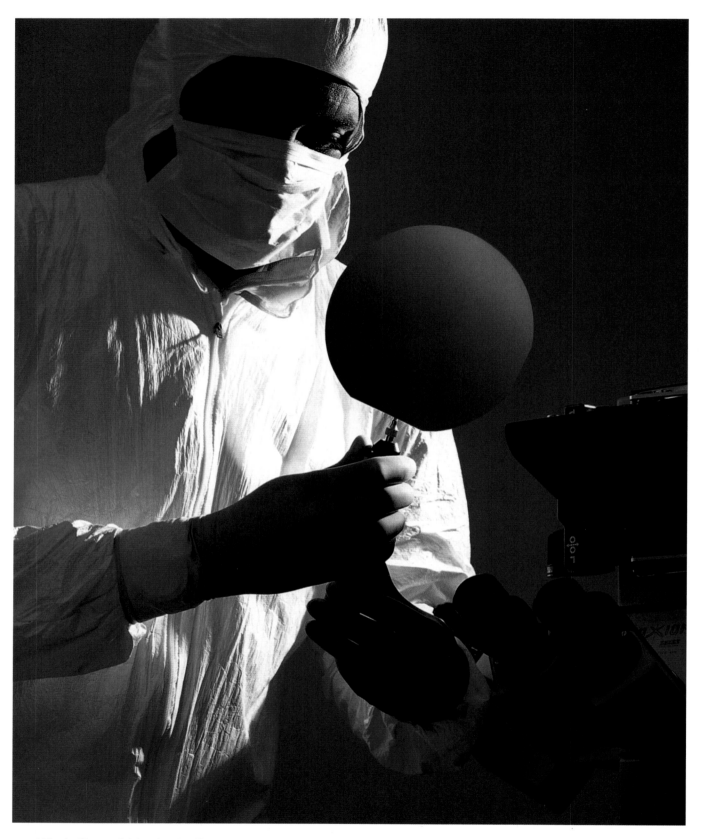

Litton's Airtron division is a leading supplier of six-inch gallium arsenide wafers for use in the telecommunications industry.

CHAPTER EIGHT

THE KEY TO VALUE

1989–1994

"The stage is now set for the separation of Litton's commercial businesses into an independent entity.... The overall plan was developed with care and deliberation. It has been put into motion at the right time."

— Orion Hoch and Al Brann, 1993[1]

PRESIDENT GEORGE BUSH appropriately described the bewildering changes that had reshaped the globe at the end of the eighties as the beginning of "a new world order." The landmark treaty signed by the United States and the Soviet Union in 1987, which eliminated intermediate-range nuclear weapons, marked a major step toward ending the arms race. Two years later, the communist government of East Germany collapsed, and the Berlin Wall, a physical manifestation of the Cold War for more than 28 years, crumbled under the hammer blows of freedom and the reunification of Germany. The Soviet Union, its economy all but dead and its ideology discredited, allowed a series of revolutions to sweep away communist regimes that governed its satellite nations in Eastern Europe. By the end of 1991, the Soviet Union had dissolved into a Commonwealth of Independent States. That same year, Bush announced drastic cuts in military spending since a Soviet invasion was "no longer a realistic threat."[2]

Cold War Fallout

The years immediately after the end of the Cold War were a difficult adjustment for Litton Industries. Starting in 1990, the United States experienced the longest economic setback since the Great Depression.[3] The recession, combined with a falling American defense budget during the late 1980s and early 1990s, had a strong negative effect on Litton's defense electronics business, especially the Applied Technology, Amecom and Guidance & Control Systems divisions.[4]

In the business jargon of the time, the result was considerable "downsizing" at Litton. To cite just one example, Guidance & Control Systems shut down an entire facility in Grants Pass, Oregon, which employed 200 people. This was part of an overall consolidation to Salt Lake City that resulted in the loss of about 650 employees in this one division.[5]

Even before the Cold War ended, Litton's executives recognized that the world was changing and had begun to cut back in areas like the Applied Technology division and the Guidance & Control Systems division.[6] In 1988, Litton had about 55,000 employees.[7] One year later, that number had fallen to not quite 51,000 employees in 40 divisions around the world.[8] Despite the drastic cuts, Litton handled the difficult task of downsizing well, for it was one of the few companies in the

---

Guidance & Control's Salt Lake City plant continued to produce laser ring gyroscopes, despite the falling defense budget.

defense electronics business that took no write-offs as a result.[9]

Litton was no stranger to cutbacks, but the reasons for these cutbacks were new. Years later, retired Litton Chairman John Leonis recalled how deep the culture shock ran when, for the first time in Litton history, viable programs that almost certainly would have gone on to be successful profit centers had to be cut back or eliminated. "I don't think most employees fully accepted that we were driven by a smaller defense budget and that the downsizing was really necessary," said Leonis.[10]

Amecom's advanced Electronic Support Measures (ESM) systems technology had enabled it to win the EA-6B Advanced Capability (ADVCAP) system in the early 1980s and the ESM system for the Navy's A-12 stealth fighter in the early 1990s. Both of these systems were near completion of their development phase when the Cold War ended, resulting in the programs being canceled for budgetary reasons.[11]

"When [former Secretary of Defense] Dick Cheney canceled Amecom's A-12 and EA-6B programs, it was a real eye opener," remembered Corporate Vice President and Treasurer Tim Paulson, who at the time had just started in Amecom as vice president of finance and administration. "It was tough being responsible for all of the finances of that division and then having to downsize it when I went in there thinking Amecom was going to be a real growth division."[12]

"After Cheney's cuts, we were down 340 employees and down to $47.5 million in sales from $150 million and growing," added Mike Gering, president of Amecom. Gering had been the marketing manager for the A-12 new business opportunity.[13]

To save jobs during this period, Amecom was able to temporarily place electronic warfare engineers at other Litton divisions. Amecom engineers added support to the Data Systems Division office at the Ingalls shipyard, to Guidance & Control's IFF product line at Northridge, California, and to Applied Technology's international business at San Jose, California.

Entire divisions were shut down due to the end of the Cold War, employees were relocated to other parts of the country as a result of the consolidations, and many employees chose to take early retirement, especially if the other option was to be let go altogether.[14]

As Leonis and other executives described it, productivity suffered along with morale as Litton Industries was forced to do more with less.[15] Litton was still well positioned for the future, but for the time being, the company did indeed reside within a "new world order."

Litton also experienced a rotation in top management during this time. When Roland Peterson stepped down as president and chief operating officer on November 1, 1990, to take early retirement,

The *Essex* (LHD-2), second in the new Wasp class of multipurpose amphibious assault ships, was christened by Lynne Cheney, married to Secretary of Defense Dick Cheney. Mr. Cheney was the principal speaker at the 1991 ceremony.

he was succeeded by Alton J. Brann, a 17-year Litton veteran from Portland, Maine, who, like most of Litton's top executives, had moved up the ladder from Guidance & Control Systems.

Brann, who held a degree in mathematics from the University of Massachusetts at Boston, joined Litton in 1973. He is credited with giving Litton more of a "commercial marketing sense," to use the words of Henry Bodurka, retired president of Litton Computer Services. "It used to be the only time you heard about Litton was in regard to the old Litton microwave oven," said Bodurka. "That changed dramatically when Al Brann took over. He opened Litton up, made it less cloak-and-dagger, if you will, and gave its marketing a higher profile."[16]

Brann was regarded by many as Hoch's successor, which was confirmed when Hoch relinquished his position as chief executive officer in 1991 to be succeeded by Brann, who became president and CEO. Hoch remained as chairman of the board, although he was shortly succeeded by Brann there too. When the low-key Hoch quietly retired, he remained on the Litton board.

Commercial Business

While some of Litton's divisions suffered from the Cold War fallout, the company's commercial side (Industrial Automation Systems and Resource Exploration Services) was faring better than ever. With occasional exceptions — such as a temporary softening in the oil business or a slowdown in automobile manufacturing, which had become one of Litton's biggest customers — Industrial Automation and Resource Exploration were the primary engines that drove Litton Industries during the immediate post–Cold War years.

In fiscal 1989, when Litton exceeded $5 billion in sales for the first time, the company credited its commercial operations as "primarily responsible for [the] higher earnings and sales."[17] The following year, oil services became Litton's top growth business.[18]

The accelerated success of Litton's commercial businesses was not a coincidence. Given the softening of business elsewhere, Litton turned to its commercial operations to help sustain growth

Western Atlas' seismic vehicles cruise through the desert in search of oil.

through a variety of acquisitions and several hundred million dollars in capital improvements.

Litton executives later said that they'd seen the changes coming as the Cold War came to a close, even if they didn't realize how fast these changes would occur. "We all knew the downturn would come, but no one knew how severe it would be," said Leonis.[19]

According to Litton's annual report, sales to the U.S. government accounted for only 45 percent of Litton's total revenues in fiscal 1990, down from 58 percent in 1987. Litton executives told shareholders that they expected the upward trend in commercial markets and the downward trend in defense markets to continue.[20]

The prediction was an accurate one. In 1991, Litton's oil field services business continued to grow. Revenue and operating profit were up 15 percent and 33 percent, respectively, with virtually all of the growth coming, as Litton said, "from international activity."[21]

Spanning the Globe

At that time, it cost, on average, half as much to find and get a barrel of oil out of the ground overseas as it did in North America, and when oil companies moved a majority of their exploration services overseas, Litton moved with them.[22]

Litton's Resource Exploration Services' annual revenues topped $1 billion for the first time in 1991,[23] and by 1992, almost 80 percent of Litton's oil field information services revenue was generated outside the United States.[24]

With the world's largest seismic fleet (30 state-of-the-art ships), Litton's Western Atlas continued to be the world leader in land and marine seismic exploration, related data processing, and core and fluid analysis.[25]

The same international thrust was occurring in the automobile manufacturing market. Litton won contracts for high-precision grinding machines from Ford of Australia and for welding assembly systems from General Motors of Europe.[26] The company had contracts with Russia's Volga Auto Works to produce and install machinery systems for engine components, and with Vauxhall Motors of England to produce an automated material handling and control system for the distribution of spare parts.[27] Litton also contracted with British automobile maker Austin Rover for an advanced manufacturing system used in the production of automobile engines.[28]

Though Litton had commercial businesses throughout Europe and some in Asia (ATAL in France, Royal in the United Kingdom, LPPI in Europe and Westrex in Japan and Hong Kong),[29] Litton's Kester Solder division helped lead the way for Litton's international presence, becoming a global supplier in the electronics industry as early as 1970, when it opened a manufacturing plant in Singapore. Over the years, Kester opened manufacturing facilities in Germany, Taiwan, Malaysia and the Philippines.

"Kester really got involved in international business probably quite some time before it was the vogue thing to do," said L.D. "Vern" Kramer, president of Kester Solder for 29 years. "Unlike a lot of the other Litton divisions that have gone overseas, we're there to serve local markets rather than import products back to the United States."[30]

The international thrust extended into virtually every area of Litton's business, in no small part because Litton had a built-in advantage when it came to dealing with international markets, one that had evolved over many years.

To service a client outside the United States, which might have ranged from a foreign government to an automobile manufacturer, Litton typically opened a facility in that country by buying an existing company. This "facility" might have been

In the early 1990s, Western Atlas added four new seismic exploration vessels to its fleet, including the *Western Monarch,* shown here. These vessels acquire data by towing multiple hydrophone-studded fiber optic cables.

A General Motors plant in Antwerp, Belgium, uses Litton's welding assembly systems in the production of car bodies.

a full-fledged manufacturing plant or merely an administrative office. As time passed, Litton used that facility as a lever to expand further in that country or region. Leonis said Litton's strategy was to have a division in every country in which it did business, no matter what that business might be, until Litton was so familiar there that it was no longer "thought of as an American company."[31]

In just one of many examples, the Litton inertial navigation system was installed on the F-104 aircraft, operated by most of the NATO-affiliated countries. As a result, Litton opened a production facility in Toronto, which eventually evolved into Litton Systems Canada (LSC), a supplier of integrated systems and a producer of sophisticated electronic equipment.

"Ever since the late fifties, Litton has been the leader in the development of inertial products as they're applied to military aircraft," said Larry Frame, a corporate senior vice president and group executive for Advanced Electronics Systems. "At the time, the military was the only customer who could afford it, so the products were developed here in Woodland Hills [California], and then other countries started using inertial systems, so we built factories overseas."[32]

Litton opened companies all over the world from Italy to Taiwan, from Greece to Saudi Arabia and from Korea to Great Britain.[33] Over the years, on the average of between 20 and 25 percent of Litton's business came from international markets.[34]

Continued Success

Despite the recession and the downturn in defense spending, most of Litton's other businesses remained profitable, and the long-term outlook was healthy. "We remained profitable during that time because we focused on being technically innovative and bringing new solutions

to places where solutions were not already in place," said Michael Brown, Litton's chairman, president and CEO in 1999. "Our goal was to do things better, faster and cheaper, and to do that, we had to drive technology, and that's what we did."[35]

In 1990, Litton Aero Products redefined industry standards when it introduced a second-generation laser gyro inertial reference system called Flagship®. The Flagship LTN-101 Global Navigation Air Data Inertial Reference System was developed for commercial application. Aerospatiale chose Flagship for installation in its new generation A330 and A340 fam-

Litton's Flagship laser gyro inertial navigation units were chosen for the Army's Apache Longbow helicopters (above) and for the European Airbus A340 (below).

ilies of aircraft and certified Flagship for installation in its other families of Airbus aircraft (A300-600, A310, A318, A319, A320 and A321). Bombardier and SAAB chose Flagship for their new regional jet aircraft. And in 1990, the French airlines UTA and Air France, along with Germany's Lufthansa, selected Flagship for their new fleets of A340 aircraft. A year later, Cathay Pacific chose the Flagship for its new A330 and A340 fleets. And by 1992, no fewer than 120 airlines worldwide were using Litton technology.[36]

Electronics continued to be an important element in the era of reduced defense budgets because new high-tech weapons platforms generally had a greater electronics content and the update of older systems was largely based on improving their electronic equipment. Litton Data Systems, for example, delivered its Tactical Air Operations Modules (TAOMs) to the U.S. Marine Corps and its derivative Modular Control Equipment (MCE) to the U.S. Air Force in the early 1990s to replace existing systems in both services. The TAOM and MCE were based on common hardware and software components tailored to the unique communications, sensor integration, and command and control needs of each service. The Marine Corps Tactical Data System replaced by the TAOM was originally developed by Data Systems in the early 1960s and then upgraded with improved data links in the 1970s. The Air Force replaced its aging Control and Reporting Centers and Forward Air Control Posts with Data Systems' new MCEs and deployed one to Aviano, Italy, where it played a key role in integrating allied communications and controlling aircraft before and during the NATO air campaign in Yugoslavia in 1999.[37]

Given its past success in upgrading electronics, Litton often found itself winning contracts to update its own equipment. In this very competitive market, it was a distinct advantage that so much of what already existed had been made by Litton Industries.

As Litton's Applied Technology division President Clayton A. Williams said at the time, "We are the incumbent on almost everything that's out there."[38]

Litton was also heavily engaged in fiber optic gyro technology navigation and was on the cutting edge of the new satellite-based Global Positioning System (GPS) for precise location

Hooded workers in a cleanroom assemble laser gyros at the Guidance & Control facility in Salt Lake City.

data. "The Global Positioning System has allowed less accurate systems to be combined with the GPS receiver to give a highly accurate navigation system without the high costs of the $100,000 units," said Darwin Beckel, president of the Guidance & Control Systems division.[39] In fiscal 1993, Litton won the contract to produce for U.S. military aircraft the first system that combined the newest laser gyro sensors and a GPS satellite receiver.[40]

Litton was on the forefront of high-speed scanning bar code technology too, thanks in part to its acquisition of the Intermec Corporation for $209 million in 1992. This technology was used to read coded symbols and was considered to be more efficient and less costly than conventional laser scanning methods. It was primarily used for stock and inventory control and became an increasingly larger part of the industrial automation side of the company.[41] The U.S. Postal Service eventually installed 2,000 of these scanners to

The first of the SA'AR 5-class corvettes was delivered to the Israeli Navy in March 1994.

automate the sorting and routing of third-class mail.[42]

The Ingalls shipyard got an international push as well. Among other projects, it built three corvettes for Israel to be used for coastal defense and control. The 281-foot, 1,275-ton corvettes were the first surface combat craft designed entirely by a computer-aided design (CAD) system linked with a computer-aided manufacturing capability that was in turn linked throughout the Ingalls shipyard.[43] "We think this corvette design significantly addresses the international market both in Asia and for Turkey, Egypt and Kuwait," Leonis told the *Wall Street Corporate Reporter.*[44]

Another sign of health came when Litton's board of directors announced a two-for-one stock split on March 12, 1992.

The Gulf War

Litton products performed brilliantly during Operation Desert Storm in 1991. While this was more of a psychological than a business boost, it was a boost nonetheless, a display of extraordinary electronic warfare capability that was seen all over the world.

The Tomahawk cruise missile, for instance, was considered a technological breakthrough due to its extreme accuracy. Litton manufactured the inertial guidance system for the Tomahawk, and that technology was combined with a terrain mapping system. Though the inertial guidance technology for the cruise missile already existed, the application of the two different technologies combined made the Tomahawk more accurate than anything before it. The mapping system's "look down" radar compared the terrain the missile passed over with what the guidance system reported it should be "seeing." If the terrain mapping system saw something different from what the guidance system said it should be seeing, the course was corrected.

The Litton Electron Devices Division (formerly the Electron Tube Division) had developed the world's first fast-warmup dispenser cathode and mixed circuit (ring loop and helix) traveling wave tube for the Patriot missiles,[45] the surface-to-air missiles famed for shooting down Iraqi-launched tactical ballistic missiles. This breakthrough enabled the division to capture essentially 100 percent of the business from that point on.[46]

Litton also implemented its high-frequency receivers in the Gulf War, which were designed to pick up radar signals with antenna arrays over a very wide geographic area. Produced by Litton's Amecom division, these antenna arrays examined signals that suggested the presence of a ship, aircraft or vehicle and determined the direction the signal was coming from and what it indicated so that counter measures could be taken.[47]

Another key system used in the Gulf War was the radar warning system, produced by Litton's Applied Technology Division (ATD). This system provided quadrant antennas, signal detection circuits and software analysis, all of which fit into a small box on the aircraft. The system alerted the pilot when a threat radar was illuminating the vehicle, and the pilot could dispense either chaff or other materials to confuse an enemy or let the warning system automatically provide for a counteraction to avoid being destroyed. This automatic counteraction could be evasive or it could emit signals to mislead whatever was illuminating the aircraft. Because the aircraft may have needed to react to signals faster than the pilot could, it was pertinent that the designers in Applied Technology were experts in incredibly fast, real-time software.[48]

"When a missile is being shot at you or an enemy aircraft is locking on with its guns or missiles, another two or three seconds sounds like a ho-hum when you're sitting in front of a piece of test equipment," explained Steve Mazzo, president of ATD. "But half a second can sometimes mean the difference between life and death.... Many of our people in this division went to Desert Storm to help install our equipment and were able to watch the effect. That kind of pride we see only as an aftermath, but it's very rewarding to know that equipment we designed performed so well."[49]

Litton also displayed its technological excellence to the world with the Airtron division's laser crystals and the Laser Systems division's range finders and target designators built with these crystals. Without the range finders and target designators, bombs dropped during the war would not have been able to find their targets.

Litton Data Systems' AN/TYQ-23 automated tactical air defense system was employed by the U.S. Marines during Desert Storm. In addition, the Navy continued to utilize Data Systems' central IFF System (AN/UPX-24) and E-2C Air Surveillance System — a technology that had been around since the 1960s — and the Army employed high-performance laptop computers and lightweight handheld terminal units, also made by Litton Data Systems, to exchange critical digital communications messages.[50]

The Navy also used all of the Litton subsystems on the Navy's E-2C airborne early warning aircraft. This consisted of the passive detection system made by Amecom, the CAINE navigation system made by Guidance & Control and the L304 central standard processing system made by Litton Data Systems.[51]

Furthermore, the military in the Persian Gulf used Amecom's Tactical Digital Facsimile (TDF) system, which provided high-resolution reproduction of military photographs that could be transmitted immediately to military officials at the Pentagon so that they could see the damage that was inflicted by U.S. aircraft on Iraqi targets. Alternatively, high resolution targeting information could be readily communicated to forward units by the Pentagon using low-grade (narrow bandwidth) communication channels. The TDF system was designed to operate reliably in the harshest environmental conditions, including salt spray, wind, rain, high/low temperature and shock. As a result of the TDF, equipment operated without failure in the extreme heat and dust of the Persian Gulf.

In all, more than 70 percent of the aircraft flown by coalition forces in the Persian Gulf War used electronic warfare equipment manufactured by Litton, and no U.S. aircraft equipped with Litton threat-warning systems was lost to radar-guided missiles.[52] Litton equipment and systems used in the Gulf War included night vision devices, laser range finders and target designators, automated artillery fire control systems, tactical air operations systems, aircraft navigation and missile guidance units, and threat warning systems, as well as destroyers, guided-missile cruisers, amphibious assault ships and modernized battleships.[53]

Though the downward trend in defense spending did not reverse as a result of the Gulf War, Litton clearly showed how important the role of advanced electronics technology was to defense. As a result, the war did much to strengthen the company's position as a leader in the defense electronics market.[54]

Litton's active-matrix liquid crystal displays (LCDs) are tested aboard a C-130 Hercules in the world's first operational demonstration of a complete aircraft LCD flight information system.

Split Decisions

Even after refocusing Litton in the 1980s, the company still served two different marketplaces with what amounted to two distinct businesses. On the one hand were the commercial businesses — natural resource exploration and industrial automation. On the other were the advanced electronics and marine engineering businesses. These various parts dealt in entirely different

marketplaces that took "a different set of skills to address," according to Leonis.[55]

In addition, dealing with both the public and the private sectors not only takes different skills but demands an entirely different attitude. Leonis pointed out that it is difficult to take a defense business culture and move it to a commercial culture. Even when some of the technology and products can be moved, such a transition demands a different management style.[56]

General Counsel John Preston explained that one reason the two are so difficult to reconcile is that people in the commercial market are concerned about price, not cost, while people in government worry about cost, not price.[57]

Larry Ball, president of Litton's Poly-Scientific division, had a finance background with commercial companies before joining Litton in 1983. "It was a very difficult transition because most of your education doesn't teach government accounting.... And it goes beyond financial. Contractual matters with the government are entirely different from dealing on a commercial basis."[58]

Because Litton's diversity made it a difficult company to analyze, the company thought itself to be undervalued by Wall Street, which it undoubtedly was, as subsequent events would prove. As one Litton executive explained, stock analysts are usually specialists, and Litton was simply too difficult and diverse for analysts to follow.[59]

But that far-reaching diversity helped explain the independent executives and divisions for which Litton was famous. It was a way of operating that worked in the 1950s and 1960s because investors liked the idea that a company could be diverse and manage risk for investors.[60] That changed as the years passed. Conventional thinking shifted to the belief that investors could and should manage diversification of assets. This led to the idea that the conglomerate structure needed modification.

Litton needed to find a way to "unlock value" for its shareholders because investing in Litton Industries was like investing in two different companies.[61]

In effect, the whole of Litton Industries was actually less than the sum of its parts at this time. Some kind of move to "unlock the value" also promised to unlock cash for Litton's military operations, cash that had been spent to build up the commercial areas.[62]

All of this had been simmering for years. Finally, the time seemed right to move. In various presentations to analysts and employees around the country, Brann and Leonis offered specific reasons for what was about to happen. They explained that Litton's aerospace/defense and commercial businesses were "non-complementary," served different markets and therefore required different strategies. In addition, the downturn in defense spending inhibited acquisitions, while the commercial businesses were strong enough to operate independently.

The Spinoff

Then, on June 18, 1993, Litton Industries announced that it would establish an entirely separate company called Western Atlas, Inc., for its resources and industrial automation businesses. It was a decision that would change the company forever.

The plan was "designed to allow the two companies — Litton Industries and Western Atlas — to implement divergent corporate strategies and to focus on different markets and opportunities."[63]

Looking back, longtime Litton executive Glen McDaniel pointed out that the Western Atlas spinoff was the natural result of a process begun many years earlier by O'Green and carried on by Hoch.

"What Fred [O'Green] did at that time was to begin the process of reconceptualizing the company, and this was carried through to completion under Orie Hoch," he said. "You might say that this

process was not completed until the much-later spinoff of Western Atlas."[64]

Both Litton Industries and Western Atlas would be listed on the New York Stock Exchange, with Litton shareholders receiving one share of Western Atlas common stock for every Litton share they owned.

At the time of the split, Western Atlas consisted of Industrial Automation Systems (Integrated Manufacturing, Material Handling and Management, and Automated Data Collection) and Oilfield Information Services (Seismic Services, Well Logging Services, Petrophysical Service and Geoscience Software).

Western Atlas had about 14,000 employees, and its fiscal year 1993 sales were over $2 billion, or would have been had it been a separate company. About 60 percent of sales came from Oilfield Information Services activities and about 40 percent from Industrial Automation Systems. The operating profit was more than $223.5 million.[65]

Over half of the revenue was generated outside the United States, with production facilities in Canada, Germany, the Netherlands, the United Kingdom and the United States, plus support and service centers in several other countries.[66]

Oilfield Information Services was, according to Litton's 1993 annual report, "a leading supplier of information technology services for the oil and gas industry" and boasted one of the largest fleets of seismic exploration vessels in the industry, including six new ships built since 1991.[67]

Industrial Automation Systems was an innovator of integrated manufacturing systems, material handling/management and automated data collection systems geared toward improving productivity, flexibility and quality. Its major customers were the global automotive and off-road vehicles industries, manufacturing, food and beverage package handling, and retail/distribution, as well as electronics and aerospace businesses. It was a primary North American supplier

Western Atlas' full-service ECLIPS well-logging system, which collects data for oil recovery, debuted in fiscal 1992. Here it is readied for precise wireline logging operations at a remote location in Venezuela.

of high-volume, integrated production systems of automotive engines and transmissions and had a firm position in the markets for welding assembly and high-precision grinding systems. It was also one of the leading companies for automated data collection systems, used for manufacturing and distribution operations.[68]

Litton Industries, on the other hand, included Marine Engineering and Production (in effect, the Ingalls shipyard) and Advanced Electronics (navigation, guidance & control; electronic warfare; command, control and communications; and components and computer products).

With about 32,000 employees, Litton's fiscal year 1993 sales would have been about $3.5 billion had it been a separate company. Coincidentally, the internal split in sales was about the same as that of Western Atlas, with Advanced Electronics accounting for about 60 percent of the sales, compared to about 40 percent for Marine Engineering and Production.[69] Operating profit was about $264 million. Its operations were located throughout the United States and in Germany, Canada and Italy.[70]

Litton's strength in aerospace/defense electronics was its "large installed equipment base and its position as a technology and market leader in a wide diversity of programs," said the 1993 annual report. It designed, developed and manufactured systems for inertial navigation and guidance; command, control and communications; and electronic warfare. Its primary customers were the U.S. military and allied nations, aerospace and defense contractors, the commercial aviation industry and civil government agencies. Also, its inertial navigation technology was used on board almost all the tactical aircraft used by the United States and allied nations. In addition, the systems were installed in land vehicles, missiles, helicopters, ships and commercial jetliners of more than 100 of the world's airlines.[71]

It wasn't until after the spinoff that Components and Computer Products (which was later renamed Electronic Components and Materials) became a product group of its own, run by Senior Vice President Donald Lepore. "Litton had always been kind of a military company," explained Lepore. "There wasn't a clear understanding of all the things we [in Components and Computer Products] were

Wireline tools are lowered into the borehole at a wellsite overseas to precisely evaluate formation characteristics.

doing. We had a hard time fitting in. But after the spinoff, we became a much larger group, started investing more in technology. And some of the divisions that had moved to other groups — like Airtron and Poly-Scientific — came back to us."[72]

Contracts with the U.S. Navy formed the bulk of Litton's Marine Engineering and Production base. (The Marine Engineering and Production group is now known as Litton Ship Systems.) Since 1975, Ingalls Shipbuilding had delivered more destroyers, cruisers and assault ships to the U.S. Navy than any other shipyard — 62 in all. And Ingalls pioneered the use of modular construction in the United States. In addition, the shipyard was constantly improving its efficiency and productivity by integrating its three-dimensional, computer-aided design with systems analysis and large-scale series production.[73]

A Difficult Transition

There is no doubt that the spinoff of Western Atlas from Litton Industries to create two different companies was a sound move financially. When it was announced in 1993, Litton stock was selling in the 47 to 48 range. Four years later, Litton stock was approaching 60, Western Atlas was well into the 80s, and Unova, a 1998 spinoff of Western Atlas that involved the industrial automation part of the company, was in the 20s. As Leonis noted, by 1998 the stock of the three companies combined to be almost 400 percent higher than the price of Litton stock alone four years earlier.[74]

For years, Litton had spent heavily on its oil services and industrial automation business, a long-term strategy to ensure the company would be strong enough to go off on its own. As a Litton spokesman said of the spinoff, "The cash flow, which has been very good on the military side, can stay on the military side."[75]

However, as might have been expected, the spinoff was difficult internally, a considerable and jarring shock to the Litton culture and to the people who worked there. What a Litton spokesman characterized as putting the final touch on the separation of the two companies came when Litton moved out of its long-time Beverly Hills headquarters and relocated to Woodland Hills in the San Fernando Valley, where Litton had a 65-acre complex that was the headquarters for several of its divisions, including Aero Products and Guidance & Control.[76]

With its ornate entrance and richly designed structure, the Beverly Hills office was famous and unique. A prime piece of real estate in one of the world's most desirable areas, it had been home to Litton Industries for 30 years and had become a

Two of the Navy's multipurpose amphibious assault ships, *Kearsarge* (LHD-3) and *Essex* (LHD-2), are shown nearing completion at Ingalls' Pascagoula shipyard.

symbol of the company. Now the new company, Western Atlas, remained there, while the old company, Litton, did the moving.[77]

Looking back at the transition, Nancy Gaymon, vice president for Human Resources, said that the sense of dislocation was profound. Many Litton employees felt that if they weren't going with Western Atlas, then something must be wrong with their performance. Of course, that wasn't true, but, as Gaymon said, it was a wrenching and emotional time.[78]

John Preston observed that one of Litton's strengths, the loyalty of its employees, actually made the spinoff even more emotional. For long-time employees, it was like breaking up a family.[79]

Management in Place

The relocation of Litton to Woodland Hills may have been the most practical move, but it was difficult nevertheless, especially when combined with the splitting of the executive management between Litton and Western Atlas.

Al Brann, who was generally given credit as the architect of the spinoff, was named the Western Atlas chairman and chief executive officer. Joseph T. Casey, Litton's vice chairman and chief financial officer since 1988, left for the same position at Western Atlas. John W. Paxton, a Litton senior vice president, went to Western Atlas as executive vice president and chief operating officer of Industrial Automation Systems. And John R. Russell, a Litton senior vice president, was named Western Atlas' executive vice president and chief operating officer of Oil Field Services.

Described as an "open communicator" and "a man with a vision," John Leonis was promoted from his position as senior vice president and group executive for Navigation, Guidance & Control Systems to become the president and CEO of Litton Industries. With the exception of a brief period with Teledyne Electronic Systems, Leonis had been with Litton since graduating from the University of Arizona in 1959 with a bachelor of science degree in electrical engineering. Brann stayed on for a time as chairman of both companies, but in 1995, Leonis succeeded Brann as Litton's chairman as well, thus

Alton Brann succeeded Orion Hoch as Litton's chief executive officer, then became the Western Atlas chairman and CEO after the spinoff.

severing the last tie between the two companies. Michael Brown was named president in 1995 and continued as chief operating officer.

Although it was announced that the spinoff would go into effect on January 1, 1994, it actually didn't become official until March 17, 1994. Most of Litton's previous annual reports lacked titles, but its 1993 annual report was named *The Next Step,* a subtle announcement that the company was entering a new phase of doing business. Litton Industries, which had gone through many incarnations in its lifetime, had reinvented itself once again.

In 1995, the U.S. Navy commissioned Ingalls to build its fourth LHD. Christened the USS *Boxer,* the ship is based in San Diego.

CHAPTER NINE

METAMORPHOSIS

1995–1997

"I think we're convinced here, and I think it's been demonstrated in the industry, that you can't take defense business culture and move it to commercial. The technologies can be moved and the products, in some cases, but you need a different culture, a different managing style."

— John Leonis, 1998[1]

THE TIMING TO SPLIT WESTERN Atlas from Litton Industries couldn't have been better. As the United States' defense budget continued to shrink, the defense industry entered an era of consolidation as defense companies competed for fewer programs and fewer dollars.

"The character and composition of the global defense industry was evolving in the face of shrinking demand," explained Litton in one 1995 summary. "U.S. defense procurements have decreased by 60 percent over the last five years. The number of U.S. defense suppliers has declined dramatically, and the remaining companies must compete vigorously on the basis of cost as well as technological excellence and quality."[2]

In 1994 the U.S. defense budget was about $249 billion, down 9 percent from the previous year. A year later the budget was about $251 billion, actually 2 percent less than the prior year with inflation taken into account and 34 percent less than 1985, the peak year since the Korean War.[3]

There seemed little doubt that Litton would rely less on defense for growth. Litton executives saw the need to expand the company's operations, moving once again into commercial and industrial markets. Or, as Darwin Beckel pointed out, "All the consolidation in the defense industry forced us to start thinking differently if we were going to grow."[4]

Teamwork

"Thinking differently" became a directive at Litton Industries during the late 1990s. Throughout its history, management had instilled a culture that George Fenimore described as "laissez-faire entrepreneurship."[5]

"I never went down to corporate unless I was forced to," said John Leonis, when remembering the corporate culture of the seventies and eighties. "If you kept your nose clean and did your job, corporate left you alone."[6]

Once he became CEO, Leonis and other Litton executives set out to change this culture while at the same time trying to increase the advancement of Litton's technology from the inside. In the fall of 1996, Leonis assigned Tom Hutchings, who at that time worked in Guidance & Control's new instrument development and who later became chief technology officer, to conduct a survey designed to increase technology synergy among divisions,

Litton supplies more than 75 percent of the world market for neodymium-doped yttrium aluminum garnet crystals, grown at a Litton facility in Charlotte, North Carolina.

eliminate any duplication of new product generation or physics generation, and combine forces to contact government technology resources. Though the results of the survey were not fully implemented until 1999, it was one of the first steps toward creating a new culture that entailed more central control from corporate.[7]

The results of the survey also led to the development of a Strategic Business Development group to tie the company's divisions closer together through exchange of personnel, streamlined processes and technology. Jim Frey was appointed corporate vice president of the group to balance, in Frey's words, "the horns of dilemma,... trying to make money available to strengthen our strong, existing core businesses and protect those properties while ensuring that we allocate some money to new areas such as information technology."[8]

Leonis also started regular meetings of an in-house organization called the President's Council, which involved the presidents from all Litton divisions meeting to share thoughts and ideas, thus reinforcing a sense of belonging to a large, multi-faceted corporation.[9]

"Though the President's Council is relatively new," said Allen J. Bernardini, president of Litton's Winchester Electronics and VEAM divisions, "it's proven to be a very good idea because it gets all of the presidents together in one room. You also get to have a direct ear to the chairman of the board and president of the corporation, so from a communication standpoint, it's superior to anything we've had before."[10]

"We try to share how we solve problems and approaches to business, and there is a lot of synergy," added Henry Bodurka, who retired from Litton Enterprise Solutions' corner office in July 1998. "It helped just to sit around and talk to the other executives. We did a lot of cross-pollination, so to speak."[11]

The result of these efforts to tie the divisions together was a gradual evolution toward a more focused company. Thirty-five-year Litton veteran Jerry St. Pé, executive vice president and COO of the Litton Ship Systems group, said that until recently, "one of the hallmarks of Litton, both in terms of its internal management style as well as how it articulated and presented itself externally, was the value of autonomy. Litton gave its business elements absolute freedom to engage in its markets. But today, Litton is moving — and properly so, by the way — toward being a more strategically focused company."[12]

Information Systems

With the downturn in defense spending, the U.S. armed services and support agencies were forced to reduce personnel while still meeting the country's defensive needs. The latest in computer and software technology enabled the creation of the information systems that made such a feat possible, allowing federal agencies and the military to do everything from monitoring terrorist groups to prison management to tracking missile targets. Such information systems also had commercial applications, allowing companies to stay competitive by automating the gathering and managing of information.

Once again, Litton was primed to take advantage of the growing reliance on information technology (IT). Since 1958, Litton had offered information systems services to the military with its Data Systems Division. The division had long positioned Litton in the IT market for military applications, developing tactical command, control, communications and intelligence (C^3I) systems that allowed commanders and their staffs to make expert and rapid decisions in tactical situations, automatically track friendly and hostile forces, control air defense weapons and sensors, and provide for close air support, interdiction, in-flight refueling and air traffic control operations.

As the Department of Defense shifted its emphasis from the development of specialized software and customized operating systems more toward the integration of global technologies into which all new systems could apply, Data Systems remained on the cutting edge of C^2 development in air defense, missile defense, naval electronics and artillery fire control.[13] The division was working not only to develop and field C^2 systems that could increase the tempo of fighting a war, but also to field its new versions faster.[14]

As an example of the scope of its technology, Data Systems designed and built C^2 centers that interfaced with an existing radar network for the entire North American continent, where numerous

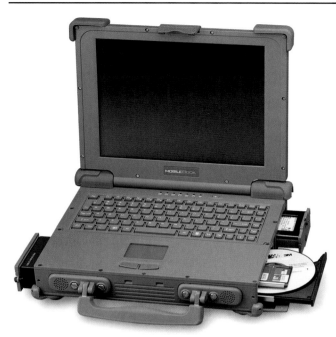

Data Systems' Rugged Notebook features a non-glare color display and is water, dust and drop proof, making it ideal for the battlefield soldier.

radar stations scanned the skies at all times. The data from these radars was then collected and analyzed by custom programs to create the most likely scenario of what was occurring in the air.[15] The technology involved in this network, like much of what Data Systems produced, was developed as a continuum of its previous technology.[16] But whereas some of the earlier air defense systems had only a 100-track capacity (a measurement of how many objects a radar can "see" at the same time), the North American air defense system required a 10,000-track capacity.[17]

One of Data Systems' key products became its ruggedized computer system modules with a flat, sunlight-readable display. These handheld units tied into a data management system so a soldier could tap into the battlefield management information grid and feed/receive information to help him carry out his mission.[18] Data Systems also began moving these sunlight-readable color display systems into law enforcement and emergency service vehicles.

To complement the division's already strong position in portable terminals for battlefield command and control, in 1997 Litton acquired SAI

Technology, which specialized in customized and ruggedized mobile computing equipment and systems.[19] "What we saw was synergy," said Frank Tullis, vice president of business development for Data Systems. "SAI Technology was building a ruggedized laptop computer unit, while at the same time, we were developing the next-generation handheld terminal unit. Plus, our briefcase-sized terminal was already comparable to their laptop computer unit. So we migrated all those products into a single center of excellence, and now ruggedized handheld computers and sunlight readable displays go to the heart of our technology."[20]

Another important technology for the division was the THAAD (Theater High-Altitude Area Defense) battle management C^3 software for the U.S. Army, which was a continuum of the technology used in the AN/TSQ-73 Missile Minder developed in the 1970s.[21] The software integrated and controlled the THAAD ground-based radar and THAAD missile in detecting and destroying theater ballistic missile threats, using "hit to kill" technology, where the system literally directed a "bullet" to intercept another "bullet" in outer space.[22]

Adding to its IT lineup, in 1996 Litton purchased PRC Inc., an information and technology services company that designed user-friendly computer-based systems for the U.S. government, commercial customers and local governments. This acquisition significantly strengthened Litton's Information Systems group, offering systems integration, software engineering, desktop outsourcing, data warehousing, weather information, information security and database design. As the world's top producer of computer-aided dispatch systems for police, fire and emergency medical services, PRC gave Litton greater access to non-defense markets.

The National Weather Service adopted PRC's interactive weather computer and communication system, called the Advanced Weather Interactive Processing System (AWIPS). This computer system essentially tied together the weather data from satellites and radar and analyzed it to produce a more accurate weather forecast. The accuracy was a result of a "much faster, more powerful computer system to analyze the data," explained PRC President Leonard Pomata.[23]

By the end of 1999, Litton expected to install more than 150 of these systems in offices around the country. The system earned the 1997 Technology Program of the Year award from *Popular Science* magazine, as well as the Smithsonian Institution's 1999 Laureate Award, which recognizes technology that improves social and community life.[24]

Pomata explained that PRC sought contracts allowing the company to provide a social service. For example, the division automated 300 million fingerprints into a digital database for the FBI, allowing agents to match a fingerprint in about 10 minutes as opposed to the 30 or 40 days it took previously.[25] Furthermore, PRC was the largest producer of 911 systems in the United States, thanks to its Altaris computer-aided-dispatch system. When someone calls 911, the odds are 70 percent in favor of a Litton system picking up the call.[26]

PRC's other key programs that would extend into the millennium included a renewed contract with the U.S. Postal Service to provide ongoing development and enhancement of its major internal automated systems. The division's Super

Litton's PRC division is the world's foremost integrator and provider of computer-aided dispatch emergency communications systems, which are found in a number of American cities.

Minicomputer Program II would provide the Department of Defense with a schedule of enterprise-wide products, service and maintenance, giving clients a single source for information technology support. And PRC won a 10-year contract to develop a government computer-based records system that would make health-related information more accessible and better protected than with paper records.[27]

PRC greatly added to and enhanced existing command, control and communications business of Data Systems. With software becoming the key component in most weapons systems, the acquisition increased Litton's share of the defense market and firmed up the share it already had, allowing Litton to compete more aggressively for contracts.[28]

Though Litton had long offered information technology services, the basic decision to begin to emphasize information technology was made not long after the Western Atlas spinoff. Senior management recognized information technology as an exploding field, not only in the government, but especially in commercial domains and federal civil domains outside of the Department of Defense.[29]

In fact, Information Systems became one of Litton's fastest-growing businesses. In the 1997 fiscal year, it contributed more than 25 percent of the company's total revenue of $4.2 billion, and Litton was named the fifth-largest federal information technology integrator by *Federal Computer Week* magazine. Information Systems had sales and service revenue of $1.3 billion in fiscal year 1997, compared to $611 million the year before. Of all the company's fast-growing information systems markets, the commercial market was growing fastest.[30]

Litton Ship Systems

Despite the downturn in defense spending, Ingalls Shipbuilding remained as strong as ever. By 1995, Ingalls had delivered 69 new destroyers, cruisers and amphibious assault ships to the U.S. Navy in 20 years, and the contracts and deliveries continued to flow. Ingalls was one of two shipyards designing and building the Arleigh Burke (DDG-51)–class Aegis guided missile destroyers for the U.S. Navy.[31]

The Arleigh Burke-class destroyers were the first U.S. destroyers in 50 years that were constructed of steel, resulting in better resistance against fire and fragments, plus protection from electromagnetic pulse.

In 1997, Ingalls was engaged in the manufacturing and refurbishing of offshore drilling rigs and production platforms, thanks to a $25 million expansion.

Ingalls also continued to build the huge LHD-class amphibious assault ships. At 40,500 tons, they were the second-largest surface-combatant ships in the Navy fleet.[32] One of the Ingalls-built LHDs, the USS *Kearsarge,* served as the base for the dramatic rescue of Air Force Captain Scott O'Grady after he was shot down over Bosnia in 1995, with helicopters dispatched from the Kearsarge instrumental in the rescue.[33]

Another sign of Litton's commitment to strengthen and broaden its commercial markets was a $25 million expansion at the Ingalls shipyard, which began in 1997.[34] At the time, Ingalls was positioning itself to build commercial vessels, offshore drilling rigs and production platforms in response to the petroleum industry's interest in deep-water exploration and production opportunities in the Gulf of Mexico.[35] Indeed, the offshore drilling in the Gulf of Mexico became "one of the hottest areas in the world," even despite a drop in oil prices, said Den Knecht.[36]

Advanced Electronics

One of Litton's first operating divisions, Guidance & Control Systems continued to develop and produce inertial navigation systems for military applications to guide aircraft, ships, land vehicles and missiles. By 1995, Litton had built well over 36,000 inertial guidance systems — more systems than all other manufacturers combined — which had been utilized by about 40 countries. With each generation, the systems became smaller, more cost effective and more reliable.

Litton's Aero Products division continued to develop and sell commercial navigation equipment, including inertial, omega and GPS navigation systems, to airframe manufacturers and airlines worldwide. Its equipment was rated highly throughout the commercial aircraft industry for accuracy, reliability, maintainability and cost of ownership. And its support organization was considered by its customers to be one of, if not the best, of its kind throughout the industry. Aero Products' equipment was also sold to U.S. and international military customers for use on transport and patrol-type aircraft such as the C-130 Hercules and the P-3 Orion.[37]

Since the late 1950s, Litton had been a leader in the development of inertial products for military applications. "At the time, the U.S. military was the only customer that could afford inertial products," said Larry Frame, senior vice president and group executive for Advanced Electronics. "So the products were developed primarily by the Guidance & Control division in Woodland Hills."[38]

By the early 1960s, Frame said, several different countries had begun employing inertial products, which led Litton to start companies in Germany, Italy and Canada. Then Litton added the 1996 acquisition of Sperry Marine, which produces marine electronic navigation and guidance systems.[39]

Further expanding Litton's product lines in guidance and control, in 1995 the company acquired Teledyne Electronic Systems, a supplier of navigation, avionics and related systems.[40] With Teledyne, Guidance & Control Systems moved into cockpit integration, which combined the inertial hardware the division had specialized in for so

GROWING THE FOUNDATION

After splitting off its oil production and industrial automation services in 1994, the new Litton Industries needed to grow, and that growth would come primarily through acquisition. It was a litany repeated over and over in press interviews, annual reports and other public statements: "growth by acquisition."

Acquisition was a sign of the times. "As the defense industry contracts, bigger companies like Litton are buying smaller ones," said one news report.[1] According to analysts, Litton's strategy of buying smaller companies allowed it to avoid higher prices and the often brutal bidding wars that were customary with defense acquisitions.[2]

Litton began by launching a series of strategic acquisitions that greatly expanded its commercial markets by purchasing Delco Systems Operations, Electro-Optical Systems and Teledyne Electronic Systems in 1995; PRC, TELDIX GmbH and Sperry Marine in 1996; and SAI Technology and Racal Marine Group in 1997. Although these new markets often did involve government contracts at some level, they were in areas other than defense and thus could be considered commercial.

For Litton, the acquisitions — or its buying "spree," as news reports put it — opened "new doors to two important markets: information technology for federal and civil purposes and marine electronics for commercial and military applications."[3]

According to one report, Litton's buying "spree" showed that "as with most companies with their roots in the defense business, Litton is trying its damnedest to diversify out of this flat and shrinking sector."[4]

In a 1996 interview, Leonis offered his own analysis, which wasn't as negative about the defense business as most newspaper and magazine reporting suggested:

"We are a technology and market leader in our principal businesses, which are defense electronics, information systems and shipbuilding.... We believe that the shipbuilding market in particular, both domestic and foreign, will grow for us over the next five years. In our primary defense marketplace we believe that U.S. procurement outlays have bottomed out, and the procurement budget should rise some through the rest of this decade, giving us good opportunities in our core businesses."

Leonis added that "defense-related revenues" accounted for about 75 percent of Litton's total revenue and predicted more "expansion in non-defense federal and local government markets and in international sales," which "we will be approaching with much more intensity."[5]

many years with Doppler radar, communications, displays, controls, identification-friend-or-foe (IFF) systems and airborne computer systems.[41]

Delco Systems Operations, also acquired in 1995, was a leading producer of inertial guidance systems for space launch vehicles and spacecraft.[42] The acquisition broadened Guidance & Control's already large base in this area and further expanded the division's technological capability with a unique product called a hemispherical resonator gyro, which was an extremely low-power-consuming, highly accurate gyro system.[43] In addition, Delco produced mechanical gyro systems for commercial aircraft, a product line that was picked up by Litton Systems Canada. The Canadian division not only considerably improved the gyro systems but also reduced their cost.[44]

With the advent of the Global Positioning System (GPS) and its ability to determine aircraft position with remarkable accuracy anywhere across the whole globe, many pundits forecasted the demise of inertial navigation systems. As the aviation industry became more familiar with the strengths and weaknesses of GPS, it became apparent that the system would need augmentation to be suitable as a Sole Means of Navigation for all phases of flight. The initial obvious weakness of GPS was its inability to provide aircraft position with sufficient availability and integrity to be suitable for aircraft operations.[45]

Responding to this deficiency, Aero Products developed an integration technology — designated Autonomous Integrity Monitored Extrapolation (AIME™). The AIME algorithm married the inertial and GPS systems in such a way that the availability, integrity and continuity of the resultant integrated system was orders of magnitude better than stand-alone GPS. The flagship LTN-101 Global Navigation Air Data Inertial Reference System incorporating AIME technology was implemented across the Airbus fleet of aircraft. Suitably equipped aircraft had the ability to descend to 250 feet anywhere in the world using only GPS and inertial sensors. Moreover, the system was able to maintain acceptable navigation performance even in the event of total loss of GPS signals. The AIME-equipped LTN-101 provided navigation performance compatible with true Sole Means of Navigation — which would allow removal of other

navigation aids (VOR/DME/ADF) from the aircraft, resulting in substantial savings to both the airframe manufacturers and aircraft operators.[46]

AIME was first developed for navigation assistance on commercial airplanes, but Tom Hutchings said that any moving vehicle could improve its performance with AIME and that it would eventually be installed on all of Litton's fiber optics and ring laser systems.[47]

The International Front

Litton was on the move internationally too, with 18 percent of the company's fiscal 1995 revenues coming from sales outside the United States.[48] In fact, by 1995, most tactical U.S. aircraft sold in the world market already had the company's navigation and radar threat warning systems installed. But Litton sought to penetrate the international market even further.[49]

Ingalls had won a contract in 1994 to modernize and upgrade two frigates for the Venezuelan Navy, another step in the shipyard's move toward gaining more international business.[50] The $315 million contract finally came to fruition four years later, once Venezuela resolved some funding difficulties.[51]

In 1997 the Industrial Development Corporation of Taiwan, Republic of China, awarded Litton a $111 million contract to supply improved radar warning receivers (RWRs) for Taiwan's new Indigenous Defense Fighter Aircraft. The system alerted pilots to the presence of hostile radar. The Italian air force also selected Litton for a $20 million contract to manufacture, test and deliver enhanced air control function modules for its command and control system.[52]

LITEF in Freiburg, Germany; its newly acquired sister operation, TELDIX, in Heidelberg, Germany; and Litton Italia in Rome, Italy, became large suppliers of electronic equipment for the multinational Eurofighter aircraft. A joint program by Germany, Great Britain, Italy and Spain, it was to include about 620 aircraft, with delivery of the first 148 scheduled between 2001 and 2005.[53]

The Litton components of the Eurofighter (valued at more than $1 million per airplane) involved a dozen pieces of advanced avionics equipment, including the attack and navigation computers that control the flow of data through the mission equipment; the inertial measurement and inertial navigation unit, which sense aircraft motion and process data for flight control and navigation; the interface processor unit; the control panel for the head-up display; and the sequencer for the ejection seat.[54] In 1999, Litton Italia won another contract for the Eurofighter to supply a Global Positioning System (GPS).[55]

Another international division, Litton Systems Canada, continued to provide semiconductor light-emitting diode (LED) displays, radar systems, and service for inertial navigation systems to the Canadian government.[56]

Litton won contracts for several integrated helicopter avionics projects. It signed to design, develop, produce and integrate the avionics package on 15 SH-2G Kaman Super Seasprite surveillance helicopters for the Australian and New Zealand navies. The package included flat panel displays, mission computers, inertial systems and control systems. Litton would also manage the inte-

gration of all avionics, weapons, communications and sensors on the helicopters.

Litton won another contract to supply an integrated avionics system for the U.S. Marine Corps AH-1W SuperCobra attack helicopter and the UH-1N Huey utility helicopter, which represented more than $600 million in potential business.[57]

Opening Doors

Another sign of the changing times in the defense industry and Litton's response to it was the push to create alliances with former competitors. "We team because we have to have horsepower behind us to get the business, to stay competitive," said Frank Marshall, Jr., associate general counsel.[58]

Litton's electronic products will be aboard all of the aircraft to be built in the Eurofighter program, helping to keep European skies secure.

As part of its international push, Litton is designing, producing and integrating the avionics package for 15 SH-2G Kaman Super Seasprite helicopters for the Australian and New Zealand navies.

Litton was reaching out to create alliances that would also open doors that might provide access to other opportunities. "In many instances, strategic alliances and teaming will be the only way that products can be made truly affordable by even the highly industrial countries," said Leonis.[59]

In a precursor to Litton's 1999 acquisition of Avondale Industries, Ingalls Shipbuilding and Avondale signed an agreement in 1997 to work together on future shipbuilding programs, both for commercial clients and for the U.S. Navy. Avondale's know-how in commercial shipbuilding would complement Ingalls' expertise in the building of combat vessels. The partnership was the first among American ship-

yards that extended beyond a single contract and was expected to make both shipyards more competitive.[60]

Also in 1997, PRC formed a strategic alliance with Hewlett-Packard to provide "computing solutions" in criminal justice and meteorology in federal, state and local markets. The alliance combined Hewlett-Packard's technical solutions with PRC's expertise in applications. PRC also entered into a partnership with the Netscape Communications Corporation, with PRC becoming the "preferred services provider for Netscape's venture into the vast federal computing market."[61]

Litton's Electronic Warfare group joined with Raytheon and Tracor to offer customized electronic warfare systems made up of off-the-shelf equipment to the international tactical aircraft market. This Advanced Self-Protection Integrated Suite (ASPIS) contained a lightweight Litton system to inform air crews of threats from radar-directed weapons. It also provided electronic countermeasure jammers to thwart hostile radar and dispensers to release chaff and flares to mislead weapons guided by radar or infrared systems. Litton signed an agreement with Greece in 1996 to equip 80 of the Hellenic Air Force's F-16 fighters with the ASPIS.[62]

Striking a Balance

No matter how much the defense industry was changing, the United States still spent more on defense than the rest of the world combined.[63] In short, opportunities in defense still existed, both in the United States and internationally, and Litton continued to develop its technology in this area.

Even with defense continuing to be a strong market for Litton, diversity remained a key ingredient to the company's success. In only a few years, Litton had built a strong presence in information technology to complement its already existing strengths in defense electronics, shipbuilding and electronic components. Such a medley of products and services would allow Litton to offset unexpected downturns in any one market, thus ensuring the company's future success. And in the last years of the millennium, Litton would increase its advantage even further by continuing to develop the corporate strategies it had already put into motion.

Litton provided much of the customized electronic warfare systems for the Hellenic Air Force's F-16 Falcon. *(Photo courtesy of* Air Force *magazine.)*

A Tactical Air Operations Center is checked out by U.S. Marine Corps personnel during a final systems test.

CHAPTER TEN

BUILDING TOWARD THE FUTURE

"We've transformed ourselves from a holding company into a more strategically and centrally directed organization. We've profitably withstood one of the most difficult federal contractor markets in decades. At the same time, we've built a balanced overall enterprise with each of our business groups gaining focus."

— Michael Brown, 1999[1]

THE WORLD OF THE LATE 1990s was faced with challenges and opportunities unique in history, as past tensions flared into new crises and former enemies embraced new ideas and open markets. On the verge of a new millennium, Litton Industries was in an enviable position and would continue to play a leading role in supplying the technology and the solutions to promote world prosperity and security.

Despite Litton's strong position in both defense and commercial markets, the last years of the millennium were filled with new challenges as the company moved to tighten the corporate reins and take advantage of growing markets.

A Shift in Leadership

In the midst of these new challenges, Litton experienced several changes in its top executives. In March 1998, the Litton board of directors elected Michael Brown as the company's chief executive officer in preparation for Leonis' retirement, "thus fulfilling its established succession plan."[2] Mike Brown had been with Litton since 1968, when he joined the Amecom division as a marketing manager. Over the years, he rose

through the corporate ranks, becoming a corporate vice president and group executive for the Electronic Warfare Systems group in 1989. In 1992, he became a senior vice president, and three years later, he was elected executive vice president and chief operating officer.

Described as "honorable," "supportive" and "committed to the success of Litton" by various Litton executives, Brown took up where Leonis left off, further moving the company into information technology and to a more centralized operating system.

Leonis passed the duties of chairman on to Brown in March 1999, when he retired at age 65, the required retirement age under Litton Industries' policy.[3] Since 1994, after the spinoff of Western Atlas, Leonis had served Litton as its president and CEO, diversifying the company into information technology and marine electronics. Announcing Leonis' retirement, Brown commended his predecessor for his many years of service. "Over a period of more than 39 years, John Leonis served this corporation in every key man-

---

This nuclear connector, produced by Litton's VEAM division, is a high-density pin-and-socket interconnect system.

In March 1999, Michael Brown (standing) succeeded John Leonis (seated) as chairman of the board after Leonis' retirement. Brown had already been appointed president and CEO.

agement position available, and he has served with distinction," Brown said. "John was instrumental in guiding and shaping Litton to be a leader in its worldwide technology markets. It is because of his insights and efforts that Litton is positioned to be successful in the coming millennium."[4]

Other changes in top management occurred also. In February 1999, D. Michael Steuert was appointed a senior vice president and chief financial officer. Previously CFO for GenCorp, Steuert held a bachelor of science in physics and a master of business administration from Carnegie-Mellon University. He was also a founding member of the Carnegie-Mellon University Council on Finance.

Harry Halamandaris was elected executive vice president and chief operating officer in March 1999. Halamandaris graduated from Utah State University with bachelor's degrees in mathematics and engineering and a master's degree in electrical engineering. He joined Litton in 1995 and had been a senior vice president and group executive for Electronic Warfare.

Extending the Reach

But even while Litton made the gradual transition into new leadership, the company continued looking ahead. To further its growth in information technology, Litton in 1998 acquired TASC, Inc., a leading provider of advanced information services and solutions to the national intelligence sector, the Department of Defense and other civil government and commercial customers.

TASC supplied a variety of computer systems engineering and technical assistance to classified, or so-called "black," government programs. The company would lend its unique scientific expertise in helping U.S. officials carry out an array of intelligence, surveillance and reconnaissance missions that were critical to national security interests. TASC's proficiency in image and signals processing also allowed military planners to get information they needed in real time to know the precise location of their forces, what the terrain looked like ahead and the latest enemy troop movements. It was called getting "information to the warfighter," and it was technology developed by TASC that allowed everyone from the soldier in the field to the Joint Chiefs of Staff or the White House to get the intelligence they needed from multiple sources to successfully plan and manage the battle.

TASC's work in modeling and simulation allowed troops to train in highly realistic virtual battlefield environments without the costs and dangers of live-fire training. TASC helped the Army develop interactive simulations that would let ground forces in Kentucky train with fighter jets out of Florida and Navy ships in the Pacific — all taking part in the same cyber battle, against the same virtual enemy, sharing the same information.

Other defense technology applications — from lifecycle engineering to analytics to database management — put TASC in the upper tier of government service providers.[5]

Weather Services International (WSI), a unit of TASC, supplied real-time weather data, imagery and forecast services to aviation, utilities, government and agricultural markets, as well as broadcast-ready weather programming and graphics systems to national media. From its own meteorological operations center, WSI provided weather information and services to 50 percent of the country's television stations, plus live, on-air reports to cable outlets such as *Fox Cable News.* Also, most major domestic airlines contracted with WSI for meteorological services.[6]

Together, TASC and PRC put Litton among the leaders in the commercial and federal weather systems markets.[7] By 1999, newscast agencies on the internet, television, radio and other media bought more than 90 percent of their weather information analysis and graphical representation from these two divisions.[8]

TASC's expertise in remote sensing, GIS and image processing also led to the operation of a precision digital imaging business for the agriculture and land-use industries. TASC could provide high-resolution digital image "mosaics" that would enable the National Forest Service to better study areas of blight or forest fires. The service, called Emerge, could analyze the color of crops and vegetation and tell farmers whether they needed more fertilizer or if they had an insect infestation, thus helping them maximize their yields.[9] In 2000, Litton management focused TASC on its core systems engineering competencies by selling WSI and Emerge.

The year 1999 proved to be a watershed year for yet another of Litton's recent acquisitions. The Data Systems unit in San Diego, acquired from SAI in 1997, made significant inroads in the law enforcement marketplace, booking orders for over a thousand of its MobileVu™ systems. Designed for use by police and sheriff jurisdictions throughout the country, MobileVu was a vehicle-mounted product that contained a Litton high-brightness,

sunlight-readable display driven by a ruggedized computer. When connected to existing radios in the vehicle, MobileVu permitted the exchange of data and images to take place over existing communications networks and greatly enhanced the peace officer's effectiveness and ability to do his job.

Several of the MobileVu successes were achieved as a direct result of the synergy between PRC's law enforcement information systems business and Data Systems' complementary product lines. The successful joint pursuits in this business area were an early result of the increased emphasis throughout Litton on identifying and exploiting such synergies.[10]

Electronic Components and Materials

Elsewhere in the company, the Electronic Components and Materials group, driven by strong demand in telecommunications, computers, medical devices and transportation, had been growing at a rapid rate throughout the late 1990s.

The group became an international supplier of connectors, multilayer circuit boards, laser crystals, solder materials and other equipment used in telecommunications, industrial and computer markets. The strong market for such components and materials increased this group's operating profit by almost 50 percent from fiscal 1997 to fiscal 1998.[11]

Altogether, this was extraordinary growth by a segment that had been relatively insignificant at the time of the Western Atlas spinoff only four years earlier. While far from the biggest group, it showed the highest profit margin and the most rapid growth.[12] In fact, several Litton divisions within the group were first or second in various markets.

"The breadth of our businesses in commercial electronics and materials makes Litton unique," Brown told investors at a 1999 conference. "No other electronics manufacturer in the world is a leader in such a variety of markets."[13]

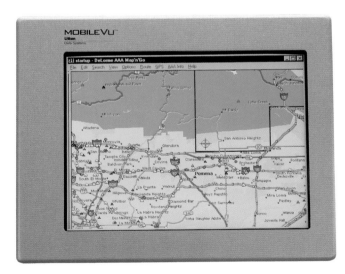

Mounted on the driver's dashboard, Litton Data Systems' MobileVu provides computer data on a full-sunlight and night-readable color display.

It was through Airtron that Litton became a world leader in gallium arsenide substrates, with Litton becoming the first company to make available six-inch gallium arsenide wafers in production quantities. "We have, over the years, passed up all the Japanese and domestic suppliers to become the number one supplier of the semi-insulating wafers in the world," said David Miller, president of Airtron.[14]

Chips fabricated from the gallium arsenide substrates had many promising electronic applications where high-speed, low-power operations were needed at higher frequencies.[15] "Most of the

The Airtron division produces and processes gallium arsenide wafers, which hold chips used in radar, telecommunications and electronic warfare systems.

gallium arsenide electronic-grade wafers go into radar systems for the military," said Miller. "They go into amplifiers for the satellites people own for direct television, and they go into cell phone amplifiers, one of the big areas."[16]

The gallium arsenide market grew in response to the increasing demand for wireless and wired telecommunication systems. Miller, who started Airtron's gallium arsenide wafer business in 1982, explained that the initial interest in gallium arsenide was for commercial amplifiers. "But then the military recognized that they could make great solid-state radar amplifier chips called MIMICs, millimeter and microwave integrated circuits. That was a very large government program that funded the development of gallium arsenide–based microwave integrated circuits. As the demand for these parts by the military started to decline, or at least moderated, the technology was directly utilized by the folks making wireless products, and so I would say today, more than 90 percent of our business is commercial based, but the demand by the military for these parts funded their development."[17]

Airtron also led the market in laser crystals. The division's new semiconductor, laser-pumped optical laser source could be used for many medical applications, including the removal of skin blemishes, surgery, removal of tooth decay and tooth enamel hardening. Industrial applications included cloth cutting, parts-making and welding.[18]

Litton's Kester Solder division, which celebrated its 100th anniversary in 1999, made Litton a leader in soldering materials for circuit boards and electronic devices. Known internationally for its quality control and customer service, Kester's soldering materials were never contaminated, as other solder companies' sometimes were. And the division became known for its solder prep materials, chemicals that help the solder adhere properly to circuit boards or other devices.[19]

Litton's Poly-Scientific division continued to design and manufacture motion technology devices for commercial and military customers. These products included slip rings, DC motors, resolvers and actuators. The division, in fact, became the world leader in slip rings. Larry Ball, president of Poly-Scientific, explained that slip rings allow for continuous rotation in such applications as providing power to heaters in rotating helicopter blades. "Without a slip ring, the wires would wrap around the shaft and eventually break," he said.[20]

The slip ring could also transmit data, a common application being CAT scan machines. The CT gantry rotates around the body, and the slip ring allows the rotation to occur without twisting wires. Slip rings have also become commonly used in security systems to allow a camera within a dome to continuously scan, thereby improving the surveillance coverage. In addition to conventional slip rings, Poly-Scientific provided fiber optic rotary joints and other optical products.[21]

The Litton Life Support (LLS) division specialized in air separation technology for aircraft application and became a leading

Above: Litton Poly-Scientific's plant in Blacksburg, Virginia, designs and builds slip rings up to 50 inches in diameter.

Below: Kester Solder, one of Litton's oldest divisions, is world renowned for its quality soldering materials.

manufacturer of onboard oxygen generating systems as well as onboard inert gas generating systems. The division was able to shrink the size of its equipment by factors of two to five while at the same time increasing throughput and decreasing cost — technological advances that won Litton Life Support several awards at the 1999 engineering symposium.[22]

"The oxygen-generating system concentrates oxygen from air," explained Kelly Coffield, LLS president. "On aircraft like the F-15E, the F-18, and the F-16, among others, the source of compressed air is the turbine of the aircraft, and once the planes have engine power, they have a device that continuously supplies oxygen to them. Without this device, the aircraft would have to carry and

replenish the supply of oxygen for the aircrew every mission."[23]

Inert-gas generating systems employ the same technology, but rather than producing oxygen from the bleed air, concentrated nitrogen is pumped into the empty space of the fuel tank as a safety measure when flying through small-arms fire. "If the oxygen levels in the space above the fuel tanks are kept below 4 percent," explained Coffield, "the tanks will not explode or burn when hit by enemy fire or when exposed to an ignition source."[24]

Litton Life Support also developed portable oxygen concentrators to treat patients at home who suffer from debilitating lung diseases, a device that won a Litton Corporate Technology Achievement Award in 1998. "Basically, this was a commercial derivative of the military technology," said Coffield.[25]

Since Litton's Advanced Circuitry, Inter-Pak Electronics and Interconnection Products divisions were joined together in 1995, they experienced compound growth and margin rates of over 20 percent, according to division president Bob Schutz.[26] By 1999, their customer base read like the Who's Who of the telecommunications, computer and networking industries.

Advanced Circuitry became the world's leading manufacturer of large printed circuit boards. Most of these were employed as the main inter-

Pilots of these Belgian F-16s breathe oxygen while flying thanks to the air separation technology of Litton's Life Support division, which manufactures onboard oxygen generating systems, as well as onboard inert-gas generating systems.

connection media to distribute voice, data and video throughout major computer systems used in the information technology markets. Along with its assembly and tester operations, Inter-Pak Electronics, with four locations in the United States, and Interconnection Products, located in Glenrothes, Scotland, provided printed circuit boards, backpanel assemblies and integrated electromechanical systems, up to and including completed switches/computers shipped right to the customer.

Winchester Electronics continued to be a worldwide provider of connector technology. The division had already enjoyed a series of "firsts" in the market, which included the first mil-grade monoblock connector, first pressurized connector, first umbilical connector, first rectangular military connector with metal enclosures and first disconnect connector.[27]

And there was more innovation on the way, according to Winchester/VEAM President Allen Bernardini. "In the future, [Winchester] will be in the forefront of producing faster speed devices, which we call matched impedance interconnect systems," he said in a 1999 interview. "The precision of the device, because of the increasingly smaller packaging, becomes very sophisticated."[28] Bernardini also had plans to move into the wireless arena, another growing market.[29]

VEAM, as well, experienced continued success as a maker of heavy-duty cylindrical electrical connectors for hostile environments. With offices in Italy, Germany and the United States, the division was also a preeminent supplier to the motion picture and entertainment industry. VEAM was number one in the world as a supplier to mass transit railed vehicles and was the first and only qualified source to the nuclear power utility industry for use in and out of containment. In 1999, the division's CIR series of connectors accounted for nearly 80 percent of its total business.[30]

The Network Access Systems division developed fiber optic communications and networking solutions, mainly for commercial markets, which were targeted at 70 percent of business in 1999.[31]

The high-quality MPEG-2 video encoders/ decoders (codecs), one of the division's three product lines, were primarily used in the higher education markets for distance learning and research — markets that demand higher-quality, lower-latency video transmission. Other markets

Winchester Electronics designs and manufactures a wide variety of rack and panel connectors.

for the MPEG-2 included telemedicine and military training.

Network Access Systems' second product line, ATM access multiplexers, transmitted data and voice at DS3 speeds over OC-12 networks and were sold to telephone carriers, military bases and other commercial businesses. These communication systems allowed bundling of cable plants, which enabled the customers to increase their offerings or utilization of the cable plant.

Finally, the division's core product line included tactical fiber optic modems that were deployed worldwide, fiber optic switchboxes for use on naval vessels, computer networking equipment designed to the Navy's SAFENET standards, and ATM circuit emulation cards used in IBM switches and bridge/router (brouters) for commercial aircraft maintenance.[32]

Opportunities in Defense

Despite the U.S. government's reduced defense budget in the nineties, 66 percent of Litton's revenue still came from federal customers and markets in 1998. By the following year, that figure had risen to 70 percent.[33] This was in part due to the government's increased reliance on information technology — an area where Litton had grown tremendously in the past few years.

Since Litton's founding in 1953, the federal market had provided the company with a stable source of revenue, even during the market's ups and downs, and Litton had proven time and again that it was a reliable provider of products, systems and services for federal markets.

But as the millennium drew to an end, the trend toward reduced defense spending began to level off, just as Litton executives had predicted. By 1999, in fact, the Department of Defense had increased its procurement budget from 3 to 5 percent,[34] with the Pentagon projecting a 25 percent rise in weapons spending by 2002.[35]

As a result of the rising defense budget, consolidations within the industry slowed dramatically. The Defense Department rejected several proposed mergers among defense industry companies, including Litton's bid to acquire Newport News Shipbuilding in 1999.

Shipbuilding

Whatever the increase in defense spending, it almost certainly promised to benefit Litton's shipbuilding segment. According to Jim Cox, a vice president and the chief financial officer for Ingalls Shipbuilding, the U.S. Navy fleet had been overtaxed for so long that not only was it in desperate need of new ships, but it also needed a great deal of maintenance of the ships that it already had.[36]

The shipyard celebrated its 60th anniversary in 1998 with a contract that had a potential value of more than $2.5 billion to build as many as eight more guided-missile destroyers of the Arleigh Burke class, which provide the primary anti-air protection for the U.S. fleet.[37]

Then, in March 1999, Ingalls signed a contract with American Classic Voyages Company for the construction of the first large cruise ships to be built in the United States in more than 40 years.[38] (Ingalls also delivered the last large American-built cruise ships, the SS *Brasil* and the SS *Argentina*, to More McCormack Lines in 1958. By 1999, both ships were still in service.)[39] The first ship was scheduled to enter service in 2003 for cruises among the Hawaiian Islands.

The new ships would be state-of-the-art, luxury cruise vessels, each about 72,000 tons and 840 feet long, with 950 cabins, a four-deck-high atrium, an 840-seat theater, a 590-seat cabaret lounge, 2,100 square feet of conference space and an outdoor performance stage.[40] George Devol, publisher of *Ocean and Cruise News* magazine, said that the two ships would most likely be the largest passenger vessels built in the United States.[41]

But building commercial ships after so many years of building military ships presented unique challenges. "When you transfer from a military design to a commercial design, many times the switch will drag with it all this mentality that's been developed over the years to create this strong combat ship rather than a commercial ship," explained Dave Wright, a vice president of Ingalls for Material/Planning.[42] In order to make the transition smoothly, Ingalls teamed with Kvaerner Masa Shipyards of Turku, Finland, one of the world's most successful and experienced designers and builders of large cruise ships.

Working with Kvaerner Masa was a prime example of Litton's synergy strategy.[43]

Also in 1999, Litton joined with Raytheon for the U.S. Navy's $20 billion DD-21 "21st Century Destroyer" program to build next generation destroyers and cruisers — a contract with a potential value to Litton of $7 billion. As part of this program, Litton would utilize the newly extended capabilities of its Computer Aided Design (CAD) system as well as implement its findings in new research and development. "We're focusing today on R&D aspects for ships that won't be built for another 10 years," said Jerry St. Pé. "This includes developing composite materials and superstructures made out of something other than aluminum, reducing manning and developing ways to prevent corrosion."[44]

Further advancing its shipbuilding business, in June 1999, Litton announced it would pur-chase the Avondale shipyard for $576.7 million. Based in New Orleans and only 100 miles from Ingalls in Pascagoula, Mississippi, the acquisition strengthened Litton's position in support vessels and commercial shipbuilding.[45]

"The two companies have complementary capabilities that provide the opportunity for what we believe are attractive synergies," said St. Pé. "We're in somewhat different markets. At Ingalls we focus on sophisticated surface combatant and large-deck amphibious assault ships, while at Avondale the focus has been more on building aux-

The Arleigh Burke-class destroyers were designed to be smaller and less expensive than the Ticonderoga-class destroyers. They also feature a broader waterplane hull, phased array radar and Vertical Launching System.

iliary ships like tankers and cargo ships for the Navy fleet. So we'll find opportunities to pursue different segments of the Navy market with our compatible capabilities and hopefully increase our success rate in the marketplace."[46]

Shortly after the announcement, St. Pé was promoted from a Litton senior vice president and president of Ingalls to executive vice president and chief operating officer of the newly formed Litton Ship Systems group. Based in Pascagoula, the new operating group was comprised of Ingalls Shipbuilding and the newly acquired Avondale.

The Avondale shipyard would be operated as a separate entity from Ingalls, but the two companies would share strategic planning and development from Litton Ship Systems. "The goal," explained St. Pé shortly after the announcement to acquire Avondale, "is to have a seamless company that is engaged in the design and construction of ships, both commercial and naval vessels, as well as a company that can provide continuing services to vessels, whether they be Navy or commercial. It's what in this industry is called a full-service contractor company."[47]

Advanced Electronics

Led by Senior Vice President Larry Frame, the Advanced Electronics group combined what was formerly known as Electronic Warfare with Navigation, Guidance & Control Systems. The result was a much bigger operating group, with its systems installed in aircraft, spacecraft, helicopters, ships, missiles, torpedoes, and land and launch vehicles.

"In electronic warfare, we're doing much more than we used to in smaller, lighter and cheaper packages," explained Halamandaris, formerly group executive for Electronic Warfare.[48] As an example, the Laser Systems division won a contract to develop the Lightweight Laser Designator Rangefinder (LLDR), to be delivered to the U.S. Army in 1999.

"This is a very substantial program that will be hugely significant both in the United States and internationally," explained Laser Systems President Robert Del Boca. "It has a multi-sensor day channel that uses a charge-couple-device type day receiver for day imagery. It has an eye-safe laser range finder and a thermal imager so you can see at night. It also has a GPS receiver and a compass so you can determine azimuth and inclination. With this system, you can fully determine anything related to target coordinates, and you can have the smart weapon follow the laser beam to the target."[49]

Another breakthrough in electronic warfare technology, according to Halamandaris, was the Amecom division's software capability for signal processing. "The key to our agreements with other contractors in supplying electronics support subsystems is not because of our hardware," he said. "It's because of our software expertise.... Now we have computer assets that allow us to determine signal characteristics in real time that in the past we did not have the ability to analyze except in an off-line mode."[50]

According to Mike Gering, the Amecom division's many patents in determining signal characteristics, including rapid precise geolocation, allowed the company not only to develop systems using much less hardware, but also to enhance the systems it already built.[51] This capability helped Amecom gain key positions on major aerospace company prime teams. Amecom, for example, became the passive electronic warfare supplier with Lockheed Sanders on the Lockheed Martin proposed Joint Strike Fighter (JSF) aircraft.

Amecom's important Electronic Support Measures (ESM) systems included the SLY-2 (V) Advanced Integrated Electronic Warfare System (AIEWS) for Navy capital ships, which replaced the SLQ-32, and the Improved Capability (ICAP-III) system for the Navy's EA-6B Tactical Jamming Aircraft.[52]

Adding to the Amecom lineup, in March 1999, Litton Industries purchased Denro, Inc., which manufactured fully digital voice and data communicating control systems and digital voice recording systems used in air traffic control and air defense applications.[53] As a result of the acquisition, Amecom became the primary domestic supplier and a major international supplier of multi-microprocessor voice-controlled switching systems. These systems were used by FAA air traffic controllers to communicate via telephone among themselves, with pilots and with others.[54]

Elsewhere in electronic warfare, Electro-Optical Systems (EOS) continued as a world leader in image-intensified night vision systems, developing and manufacturing almost all varieties of the image-intensified night vision systems that the U.S. Army has fielded over the last 25 years, according to EOS President Steven Lambert.[55] In fact, EOS won the largest share of the U.S. Army's Omnibus V night vision equipment program in 1998.[56] In addition, EOS was one of only two qualified producers in the United States for laser protection filters. These filters protected against all kinds of lasers, which could damage or blind equipment.

Another new EOS technology completely eliminated unwanted reflections and fogging of the image, referred to as flare or blooming. "On most of the night vision devices, if a very bright object comes into view, you see an after-image if the camera or object is moving," explained Hutchings. "This new technology eliminates that, and this is a real boon for many applications, including police, anti-terrorism units, the military, and local, state and federal governments.... For instance, if you have a fire situation with potential casualties, the flare from the house fire won't dim the night vision wearer's view. So if anyone is lying on the ground near the fire, the flare won't hide the victim."[57]

Guidance & Control's new micro-electro-mechanical devices (MEMs) — which were also being developed at Poly-Scientific and LITEF — were extremely important to future products. These miniature devices combined a host of electronics and sensors into a miniature package that could do acceleration detection and rotation sensing in navigation devices. Essentially, they were miniature gyros and accelerometers. MEMs could also be adapted for chemical, biological, temperature and pressure sensors. By 1999, MEM devices were being put into all of Litton's inertial navigation systems, and the company had several exploratory programs to put them into optical switches for the communications business.[58]

In addition to already supplying the main computer, attitude heading reference unit, emitter location processor and data communications devices for the European Tornado aircraft, LITEF and Litton Italia updated the Tornado by supply-

The Electro-Optical Systems division's night vision goggles are provided to both military and law enforcement personnel.

ing the inertial navigation unit and various missile launch control computers.

The Electron Devices Division (EDD) continued to be a leader in the design and production of state-of-the-art vacuum electron devices (VEDs). VED performance typically drives electromagnetic system performance; hence, novel devices and innovation originating from EDD were key to fielded system upgrades and more capable future systems.[59]

For example, EDD developed a unique folded waveguide traveling wave tube that was ideal for high-power radar and communication systems. The division also developed a new type of clustered cavity broadband klystron for the AWACS

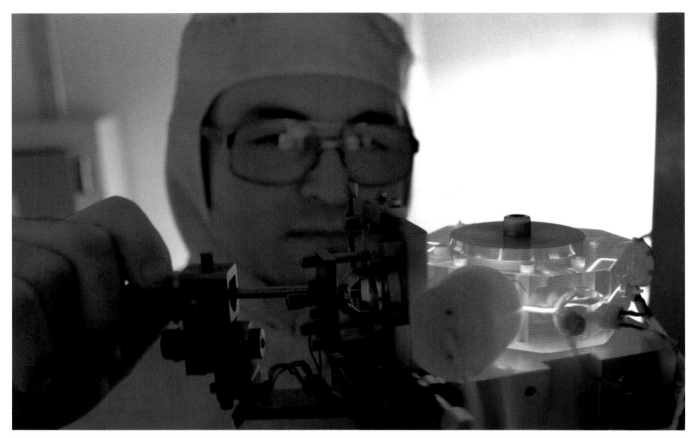

The Guidance & Control Systems division's ring laser gyroscopes are critical elements of precision for guidance and control of ships, missiles, spacecraft and aircraft.

radar system, which covered the whole band with one device rather than two, and a novel hollow electron beam current regulating switch tube for use in high-power modulators.[60]

Teaming up with Communications and Power Industries, the Naval Research Lab and the University of Maryland, EDD developed and demonstrated a 94 ghz gyroklystron amplifier capable of pumping out over 100,000 watts of peak power and 10,000 watts of average power.[61] This device was to be used in a new high-resolution radar system.

On the commercial side, EDD's klystrons were used in airport surveillance and weather radars and as RF power sources for medical linear accelerators used in treatment of cancer and in UHF TV transmitters.[62]

And the division engineered a new television transmitter tube that should cut power requirements by nearly a factor of 2.5. It was estimated that this would save the United States hundreds of millions of dollars in power over the next five years and could also be applied to military products. The invention won the 1999 Thornton Award, which is Litton's highest honor for new technology developments.[63]

In 1996, Litton had added the highly respected Sperry Marine to its advanced electronics portfolio, making Litton the world's largest producer of marine electronic navigation and guidance systems for both commercial and military customers, including automated and integrated ship bridge systems. These bridge systems were much like a control tower for aircraft, integrating all the consoles on a color display that showed the working functions of the ship, the terrain around the ship and weather conditions. The bridge also included radio systems, a ring laser gyro inertial navigation system and radar systems — all sold through Sperry Marine.[64]

The Litton-integrated bridge system was a principal part of the U.S. Navy's first "Smart Ship," the USS *Yorktown*, which was designed to "provide a significant reduction in manning requirements" while maintaining safety and operational standards. Litton's integrated bridge system automated data gathering and many other ship operating tasks, which both reduced the manpower needed to run the ship and allowed the crew to concentrate on navigation and other high-priority tasks.[65] Litton's systems, along with changes in operating policies and procedures, allowed for a 15 percent reduction in the *Yorktown*'s crew.[66]

Sperry Marine, along with C. Plath, Decca Marine and the Racal Marine Group, comprised the Litton Marine Systems division. This division provided "Total Ship Systems Solutions" with involvement in every cycle of a ship's life — from design and construction to supplying systems and components to providing maintenance expertise. Because Sperry's equipment was installed on ships all over the world, it maintained 24-hour service facilities for vehicle support anywhere on the globe. The company even offered the U.S. Navy a proposal to take advantage of Sperry's 24-hour service by outsourcing all its vehicle maintenance to Litton, thus saving time and money.[67]

Sperry Marine won an important contract in March 1998, making it the first company to supply AN/WSN-7 ring laser gyro systems for U.S. Navy surface ships and submarines. The system provided precision location in digital and analog formats and would replace existing gyro navigation systems used on aircraft carriers, attack submarines and surface combat ships.[68]

Litton also began focusing more on its aerospace businesses. As a reaction to Department of Defense downsizing, Amecom offered contract engineering design and manufacturing services for aerospace electronic applications. It built power supplies and data handling systems for NASA and by 1999 had delivered more than 200 printed wiring board assemblies with dozens of different designs, including boards on the Hubble repair mission. "We provide NASA with design work, auditing of designs, and help with various engineering tasks," explained Mike Gering.[69]

Amecom was also building the avionics bus for the *Earth Orbit 1* satellite, which, in Gering's words, "is essentially the brains of the satellite."[70] Additionally, Amecom manufactured UHF radios for NASA. These radios were installed on the space shuttle, the space station and the astronauts' Extravehicular (EVA) pack. They first flew on the STS 95 mission in 1998 on which John Glenn returned to space. Amecom designed and built the UHF antennas used with these radios as well. This antenna design was later adapted for the Mars 1998 and 2001 landers and orbiters. Additional orders were received for UHF antennas for the shuttle and space station's Wireless Video System (WVS).[71]

In addition, Amecom began developing a very small, ultra-low-power Miniature Satellite Threat Reporting System (MSTRS) that detected interference with DOD satellites and had the potential for application to commercial satellites. The first flight tests were scheduled for December 2000 on shuttle flight number STS-107 and on the Mighty SAT 2.2 satellite in October 2001.[72]

Other space endeavors included a 1998 contract to develop and manufacture the gyro reference assembly for the U.S. Air Force's Space-Based Infrared System, which would eventually replace the current missile warning system. Litton's system would allow the spacecraft to track missiles with high-precision accuracy. In addition, Litton was contracted to design a fiber optic gyro inertial reference unit that would be resistant to the radiation often encountered in space.

Litton's newly formed Spacecraft Electronics virtual company — made up of various Litton divisions including Guidance & Control, TELDIX and Amecom — could supply an entire vehicular control stabilization subsystem to a prime company.[73]

A Sharper Focus

While Litton continued to focus on its technology, the company was also transforming itself from a financially controlled company to a strategically controlled company, which included more direction from senior management.

To that end, in the spring of 1999, Litton began implementing a progressive program based on six initiatives designed to create value. Litton management would now concentrate on what it described as the six elements to profitable growth: employee development, synergism among divisions, productivity improvement, excellence in technology, market-focused growth and value metrics methodology.

In truth, Litton was putting a name to what it had already set in motion, only now the company had a system to measure the value it created and to support that growth through appropriate planning and compensation programs. And though the initiatives had been suggested as "good things to do" several years prior, the company now required every division president to incorporate aspects of them into their planning process for fiscal year 2000.[74]

Employee Development

One of the strategies Litton planned to implement was to further develop its people. The company took two approaches to achieve this. First, it sought to make an environment in which employees were continuously learning and improving. This included providing employees with the proper tools, developing a stellar human resources team and training management to provide ample support.[75] Many of Litton's divisions had already begun implementing "principle centered leadership" — the idea that everyone, at all levels, must perform their jobs to the best of their abilities and integrate those jobs in order to maximize performance.[76] Furthermore, all of the Litton divisions sought to provide active training programs at all levels, which would continuously be reviewed and improved.[77]

Secondly, Litton began enforcing a management succession plan to ensure that the company would always benefit from good management. This meant more training in areas where employees formerly may not have been trained. A strong technologist who showed potential for

This Panavia Tornado in Royal Air Force camouflage is equipped with TELDIX's ultramodern display system. *(Photo courtesy of* Air Force *magazine.)*

making good business decisions, for example, might be trained in contracts, business law, international business and marketing, thus creating a future potential candidate for a senior management position.[78]

Synergy

Creating more corporate synergy became another of Litton's strategic goals. "Litton's culture is always evolving," said John Preston. "The culture of Litton today is dramatically different from what it was 10 years ago. It's been an evolution, sometimes driven by business needs, sometimes driven simply by personalities of the people in top positions."[79]

Business needs and the personalities of Litton's executives led to the push for more synergy. "After three years of trying to change this culture," said Leonis in a 1998 interview, "we're finally beginning to see some really productive things where we get the synergies from all of the businesses we have. That way we're not just a holding company with companies here, here, and here."[80]

In essence, the synergism among Litton's divisions allowed the company to offer systems that built on each other, thus allowing Litton to offer complete technological solutions. During the Bosnia air campaign, the U.S. Air Force issued an urgent requirement, which became known as the Sure Strike program, for which Litton combined Laser Systems' laser target-designation technology, Electro-Optical's night-vision technology, Guidance & Control's guidance technology and Data Systems' handheld terminal technology to provide F-16 aircraft with the precision location and target-cueing capability that allowed first-pass delivery of weapons with pinpoint accuracy.

In another example of synergy, TASC coupled its weather expertise with Data Systems' command and control systems expertise to combat chemical biological warfare, creating a product for a joint service program. "There are two critical ingredients to chemical biological problems," said Frank Tullis of Litton Data Systems. "First, you have to know you have a problem, and that's a function of sensors, and that's where our expertise comes in. Then, the problem is mostly influenced by weather — the winds and rain and so

forth — and that's where TASC's technology comes in. We married the two technologies so that any unit, whether it's an air base, a ship, or a battalion, could be quickly aware of the problem and know what its long-term implications are for them and their maneuvers."[81]

Furthermore, Sperry Marine combined its naval inertial navigation system business with LITEF's naval group to win nearly 80 percent of all international contracts for naval inertial navigation systems in the countries where they were allowed to export. The actual breakdown of the market share had Sperry Marine with 47 percent, LITEF's naval group with 31 percent, Raytheon with 11 percent and Sagem with 11 percent.[82]

As of spring 1999, Litton Industries had four robust and dependable product groups or "segments," as they were sometimes called. Such an organizational structure allowed Litton to more effectively manage its core competencies. Each of the four groups — Information Systems, Electronic Components and Materials, Advanced Electronics Systems, and Litton Ship Systems — was made up of Litton divisions.

Reported one industry publication, "The outcome [of Litton's organizational structure] has been a corporate headquarters leading a family of competencies that Litton provides best, instead of a flagship unit managing only 'companies' via the traditional results-oriented approach, which is often slow to trim sails while attaining direction and speed."[83]

Litton added to the increased sense of teamwork by forming teams, or "virtual companies," made up of management from corporate and the various divisions, to discuss strategic initiatives, where they were, where they wanted to go, and how best to get there. Litton described the virtual company as "an internal linkage of the product and services capabilities of several divisions." Nancy Gaymon acknowledged this horizontal integration as "a big change for the company."[84]

The company created three such virtual companies, one each for Ship Systems, C4ISR, and Spacecraft Electronics. Each virtual company includes several divisions, sharing their components to create an integrated system, which would allow Litton to better compete against larger companies. In addition to customers buying compo-

As this brochure for Litton Data Systems indicates, Litton's technology is always building toward the future.

nents from each division, Litton could offer an entire product, which simplified customer use.[85]

"In business, teamwork is critical," Mike Brown told a symposium of engineers. "To a large degree, individual performance must be set aside. Not entirely, of course. But a considerable part of the secret of success in business today is the ability to form teams.... Teamwork actually stimulates the kind of technological creativity we value at Litton, resulting in practical, workable solutions that bring results to our company, our customers and our shareholders."[86]

Productivity Improvement

One of the qualities that always distinguished Litton was its strong manufacturing base — the ability to manufacture what it engineers. "Litton is a high-technology manufacturing company — not just high technology," said Joseph Caligiuri. "When I came to Litton [in 1969], that was the thing I was so delighted about. I came from a great engineering organization but a poor manufacturing organization, and here was Litton Industries, which knew how to put into production configuration very sophisticated technological systems."[87]

Despite such a strong manufacturing base, Litton still saw room for refinement, which is why one of its six new initiatives focused on productivity improvement. The goal of this initiative was to review all of the company's production, quality control, procurement, personnel management and training programs to determine which methodologies and processes worked best. The survey that Hutchings conducted in 1996 revealed that about 60 different processes were being used throughout the divisions. And while many of them were similar, Litton's goal was to filter out those processes that didn't work and focus on those that did so that all the divisions had access to methods that would improve their productivity.[88]

Technological Excellence

Achieving and maintaining world-class technological excellence had been one of Litton's goals since the company's founding. To help foster that commitment, at the 1999 President's Council, Brown and the other members of senior management announced a new technical excellence initiative led by Halamandaris that would help Litton take technology "to the next level."[89] The goal of this sharper focus on technology was to ultimately assure technological leadership in all of Litton's markets. "We're going to treat what we might call technology management as a business," Brown said.[90]

One goal of the technological excellence initiative was to concentrate on new techniques and methodologies that would replace products with better, newer technologies. Litton also established a Chief Technology Officer Council, led by Tom Hutchings, to tie together the technologists throughout the corporation, sharing ideas and projecting new markets based on emerging technologies.

Litton believed that technologists, by the very nature of their business, contributed to advanced projections of where the world was headed and, consequently, where Litton needed to focus its efforts. Each division was required to project how each of its products would fare in one-year, three-year and five-year projection plans. Finally, the projections were tied closely to the sales and marketing plan so that, in Hutchings' words, "We have the right technology at the right time."[91]

Wise Investments

Litton also planned to make market-focused investments, which meant adopting a new methodology that assessed whether divisions were investing their money in areas that would yield the maximum and most beneficial marketing position in the future. A market focus group at the corporate level would review the projections made by divisions and decide whether the investments were suitable, whether a particular product needed to be pushed faster due to a fast-growing market, or whether to increase or decrease the emphasis in a specific market.[92]

On the financial side, the value metrics strategy measured the company's success by cash flow return-on-investment, which CFO Michael Steuert said would "provide the company with a very accurate comparison to its cost of capital."[93] When Litton first adopted value metrics, the company's cash flow return-on-investment was equal to its cost of capital. Litton's long-term goal was to generate a return of at least 3 percent over the cost of capital for the company, along with double-digit growth.[94] Litton also planned to generate free cash flow to use for acquisition and growth, debt repayment or repurchasing of shares. Steuert said he expected the cash flow return-on-investment value metrics strategy to accelerate the company's returns over the next several years.[95]

Poised for Success

Despite a whirlwind of change, Litton ended the century with a strong foundation for the future. By 1999, the company held over 2,000 patents and had established an office of technology and licensing to both preserve and exploit its technological advances.[96] Furthermore, Litton Industries had positioned itself to take advantage of business opportunities by extending its holdings in shipbuilding, information systems, and electronic components and materials. Management focused its efforts on increasing value with thoughtful allocation of capital, honing its strengths in management and teamwork, and continuing its drive to be a technical leader in all of its markets.

"We're in a lot of different markets, a lot of different technologies and application areas of expertise," said Brown. "And in every one of those, we've seen the same kind of push for technical excellence, ... whether it be in electronics, fiber optics, electronic warfare, shipbuilding techniques or information systems. Litton can be extremely proud that in most of these diverse companies, diverse markets, diverse technologies, we're number one or number two in the world."[97]

A TIMELINE OF KEY EVENTS IN THE

Litton Industries is originally founded by Charles Bates Thornton as Electro Dynamics Corp. in November 1953. One month later, the company changes its name to Litton Industries after acquiring a small electron tube company from Charles Litton.

On July 30, 1957, Litton Industries is listed on the New York Stock Exchange.

Litton acquires Western Geophysical Company of America in 1960, giving Litton a strong position in seismic exploration.

Litton's lightweight inertial navigation system for aircraft becomes operational in 1958, paving the way for Litton's future success in that area.

1945	1950	1955	1960	1965	1970

In 1961, the company purchases Ingalls Shipbuilding Corporation, which paves the way for Litton's stellar success in ship-building.

In 1968, the Ingalls shipyard begins construction of a new facility for modular construction of ships, a method that Ingalls pioneered in the United States.

In 1972, Fred O'Green succeeds Roy Ash as president of Litton Industries and begins restructuring the company to greater profitability by focusing on high technology.

EVOLUTION OF LITTON INDUSTRIES

In the early 1980s, Litton divests itself of companies that do not relate to its core businesses, including the entire Business Systems segment.

Orion Hoch succeeds O'Green as Litton's CEO in 1986. Two years later, O'Green retires as chairman of the board and Roland Peterson is elected president.

In 1985, Litton begins a stock buyback program to eliminate its dividend, thus protecting itself against hostile takeover attempts.

In 1987, Litton combines its Resources group and the Atlas division to create a new subsidiary, Western Atlas International.

| 1975 | 1980 | 1985 | 1990 | 1995 | 2000 |

Roland Peterson passes the presidential reins to Alton Brann in 1990.

In 1994, the company separates its commercial businesses by spinning off Western Atlas from Litton Industries, thus creating two separate companies.

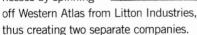

Michael Brown is elected CEO in 1998 and becomes chairman of the board the following year upon Leonis' retirement.

John Leonis is appointed president and CEO of Litton in 1993.

In the mid to late 1990s, Litton makes a flurry of acquisitions to strengthen its presence in information systems, marine electronics and commercial electronics.

In 1999, Litton acquires the Avondale shipyard, thus strengthening its position in support vessels and shipbuilding.

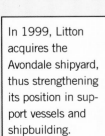

NOTES TO SOURCES

Chapter One

1. "Man with a Plan." *Time* (Sept. 15, 1958).
2. Halberstam, David. *The Reckoning*, p. 204.
3. "An Appetite for the Future." *Time* (Oct. 4, 1963): p. 106.
4. Byrne, John A. *The Whiz Kids.* New York: Currency Doubleday, 1993, p. 44.
5. Ibid., p. 50.
6. Halberstam, David. *The Reckoning*, p. 205.
7. Byrne, John A. *The Whiz Kids.* New York: Currency Doubleday, 1993, p. 51.
8. Lay, Beirne, Jr. *Someone Has to Make It Happen.* Prentice-Hall, p. 78.
9. The United States Chamber of Commerce.
10. The Ford Motor Company archives.
11. Lay, Beirne, Jr. *Someone Has to Make It Happen.* Prentice-Hall, p. 87.
12. Byrne, John A. *The Whiz Kids.* New York: Currency Doubleday, 1993, p. 146.
13. Murphy, Charles J.V. "The Blowup at Hughes Aircraft." *Fortune* (Feb. 1954).
14. Byrne, John A. *The Whiz Kids.* New York: Currency Doubleday, 1993, p. 236.
15. Glen McDaniel, interviewed by Bob Wisehart, Aug. 17, 1998, transcript p. 5.
16. Ibid.
17. Murphy, Charles J.V. "The Blowup at Hughes Aircraft." *Fortune* (Feb. 1954).
18. Ibid.
19. Byrne, John A. *The Whiz Kids.* New York: Currency Doubleday, 1993, p. 241.
20. Murphy, Charles J.V. "The Blowup at Hughes Aircraft." *Fortune* (Feb. 1954).

Chapter Two

1. "Background Information on Litton Industries," Litton Industries Public Relations Department, Beverly Hills, CA, 1961, p. 2.
2. "Man on the Move." *Forbes* (July 15, 1961): p. 15.
3. Glen McDaniel, interviewed by Bob Wisehart, Aug. 17, 1998, transcript pp. 5–6.
4. Ibid., p. 12.
5. Lay, Beirne, Jr. *Someone Has to Make It Happen.* Prentice-Hall, p. 128.
6. Byrne, John A. *The Whiz Kids.* New York: Currency Doubleday, 1993, p. 287.
7. "An Appetite for the Future." *Time* (Oct. 4, 1963): p. 107.
8. "Man with a Plan." *Time* (Sept. 15, 1958).
9. Glen McDaniel, interviewed by Bob Wisehart, Aug. 17, 1998, transcript p. 8.
10. Ibid., p. 12.
11. Lay, Beirne, Jr. *Someone Has to Make It Happen.* Prentice-Hall, p. 132.

12. Litton Industries 1954 Annual Report.
13. Glen McDaniel, interviewed by Bob Wisehart, Aug. 17, 1998, transcript p. 8.
14. Litton Industries 1954 Annual Report.
15. Ibid.
16. "An Appetite for the Future." *Time* (Oct. 4, 1963): p. 104.

Chapter Two Sidebar

1. Weiner, Jack B. "The Management of Litton Industries." *Dun's Review* (May 1966).
2. Byrne, John A. *The Whiz Kids.* New York: Currency Doubleday, 1993, p. 290.
3. Litton Industries archives.
4. Weiner, Jack B. "The Management of Litton Industries." *Dun's Review* (May 1966).
5 Lay, Beirne, Jr. *Someone Has to Make It Happen.* Prentice-Hall, p. 126.
6. Ibid., pp. 126–127.

Chapter Three

1. "Man with a Plan." *Time* (Sept. 15, 1958).
2. "Man on the Move." *Forbes* (July 15, 1961): p. 16.
3. Lay, Beirne, Jr. *Someone Has to Make It Happen.* Prentice-Hall, p. 132.
4. Tindall, George B. and David E. Shi. *America.* 2nd ed. New York: W. W.

Norton & Company, 1989, pp. 794–802.
5. *Khrushchev Remembers: The Last Testament.* Edited and translated by Strobe Talbot. Boston: Little, Brown, 1974, p. 54.
6. Litton Industries 1959 Annual Report.
7. Ibid.
8. Glen McDaniel, interviewed by Bob Wisehart, Aug. 17, 1998, transcript p. 12.
9. "Man on the Move." *Forbes* (July 15, 1961): p. 16.
10. George Fenimore, interviewed by Bob Wisehart, May 28, 1998, transcript p. 38.
11. "Litton Profits Exceed One Million," Litton news release, 1956.
12. Litton Industries news release, Monday, July 29, 1957.
13. "Man With a Plan." *Time* (Sept. 15, 1958).
14. "Man on the Move." *Forbes* (July 15, 1961): p. 15.
15. "An Appetite for the Future." *Time* (Oct. 4, 1963).
16. Rieser, Carl. "When the Crowd Goes One Way, Litton Goes the Other." *Fortune* (May 1963).
17. Information provided by Dr. Richard True, Electron Devices Division, Oct. 28, 1999.
18. Information provided by Richard George, Data Systems Division, Sept. 7, 1999.
19. Ibid.
20. Ibid.

21. Litton Industries 1956 Annual Report.
22. Ibid.
23. Litton Industries 1958 Annual Report.
24. Litton Industries 1959 Annual Report.
25. Information provided by Richard Hopman, LITEF division, Sept. 29, 1999.
26. Robert Knapp, interviewed by Pat Prince Rose, May 18, 1998, transcript p. 38.
27. *Airline Executive* magazine (Nov. 1983).
28. "An Appetite for the Future." *Time* (Oct. 4, 1963).
29. "Man on the Move." *Forbes* (July 15, 1961): 15.
30. Information provided by Richard George, Data Systems Division, Sept. 7, 1999.
31. Ibid.
32. Ibid.
33. Ibid.
34. Glen McDaniel, interviewed by Bob Wisehart, Aug. 17, 1998, transcript p. 15.
35. Rieser, Carl. "When the Crowd Goes One Way Litton Goes the Other." *Fortune* (May 1963).
36. Litton Industries 1958 Annual Report.
37. Glen McDaniel, interviewed by Bob Wisehart, Aug. 17, 1998, transcript p. 15.
38. "Man on the Move." *Forbes* (July 15, 1961): p. 15.
39. Litton Industries archives.

40. Standard & Poor's memorandum, March 13, 1958.
41. "Man on the Move." *Forbes* (July 15, 1961): p. 18.
42. Litton Industries 1958 Annual Report.
43. Glen McDaniel, interviewed by Bob Wisehart, Aug. 17, 1998, transcript p. 28.
44. Ibid.
45. Ibid.
46. Ibid., p. 32.
47. Litton Industries 1959 Annual Report.
48. "Man on the Move." *Forbes* (July 15, 1961): p. 18.
49. Litton Industries 1956 Annual Report.
50. Litton Industries 1959 Annual Report.

Chapter Four

1. Litton Industries 1961 Annual Report.
2. Byrne, John A. *The Whiz Kids.* New York: Currency Doubleday, 1993, p. 380.
3. Litton Industries 1960 Annual Report.
4. "An Appetite for the Future." *Time* (Oct. 4, 1963): p. 104.
5. "The Management of Litton Industries." *Dun's Review* (May 1966).
6. Ibid.
7. "An Appetite for the Future." *Time* (Oct. 4, 1963): p. 104.
8. "What Puts the Whiz in Litton's Fast Growth." *Business Week* (April 16, 1966).

9. Byrne, John A. *The Whiz Kids*. New York: Currency Doubleday, 1993, p. 385.
10. George Fenimore, interviewed by Bob Wisehart, Sept. 1, 1998, transcript p. 25.
11. Ibid.
12. Glen McDaniel, interviewed by Bob Wisehart, Aug. 17, 1998, transcript pp. 47–48.
13. Litton Industries 1961 Annual Report.
14. Ibid.
15. Litton Industries news release, March 1, 1960.
16. "An Appetite for the Future." *Time* (Oct. 4, 1963): p. 109.
17. "The Management of Litton Industries." *Dun's Review* (May 1966).
18. Rieser, Carl. "When the Crowd Goes One Way Litton Goes the Other." *Fortune* (May 1963).
19. Ibid.
20. "Technology of War," *Encyclopedia Britannica*. Volume 29, Macropædia (Chicago) pp. 604–605.
21. "Another Submarine Seen off California." *New York Times* (April 2, 1950).
22. Litton Industries 1962 Annual Report.
23. Lay, Beirne, Jr. *Someone Has to Make It Happen*. Prentice-Hall, p. 166.
24. Information provided by Dr. Richard True, Electron Devices Division, Oct. 28, 1999.
25. Litton Industries 1962 Annual Report.
26. Ibid.

27. Allward, Maurice, Michael Heatley, Mark Hewish, and Andy Hofton. Edited by Bill Gunston. *The Encyclopedia of World Air Power*. London: Crescent Books, 1980, p. 186.
28. Litton Industries 1963 Annual Report; Frank Tullis, interviewed by Melody Maysonet, Aug. 4, 1999, transcript p. 4.
29. Frank Tullis, interviewed by Melody Maysonet, Aug. 4, 1999, transcript pp. 4, 5.
30. Litton Industries 1964 and 1965 annual reports.
31. Litton Industries 1966 Annual Report.
32. Rieser, Carl. "When the Crowd Goes One Way, Litton Goes the Other." *Fortune* (May 1963).
33. Information provided by Allen J. Bernardini, Winchester and VEAM divisions.
34. Ibid.
35. Information provided by Allan R. Baron, Advanced Technology group, Sept. 3, 1999.
36. Litton Industries 1966 Annual Report.
37. Lay, Beirne, Jr. *Someone Has to Make It Happen*. Prentice-Hall, p. 171.
38. Ibid., p. 169.
39. Byrne, John A. *The Whiz Kids*. New York: Currency Doubleday, 1993, p. 387.
40. Litton Industries 1965 Annual Report.
41. Litton Industries 1967 Annual Report.

42. "The Management of Litton Industries." *Dun's Review* (May 1966).
43. Speech by Crosby Kelly, Litton archives.
44. "The Management of Litton Industries." *Dun's Review* (May 1966).
45. "An Appetite for the Future." *Time* (Oct. 4, 1963).
46. George Fenimore, interviewed by Bob Wisehart, Aug. 31, 1998.
47. "Management Talks to Roy Ash." *Management: The UCLA Graduate School of Management Magazine* (Spring 1984): p. 6.
48. "What Puts the Whiz in Litton's Fast Growth." *Business Week* (April 16, 1966).
49. Ibid.
50. Robert Knapp, interviewed by Pat Prince Rose, May 18, 1998, transcript p. 6.
51. "What Puts the Whiz in Litton's Fast Growth." *Business Week* (April 16, 1966).
52. "The Management of Litton Industries." *Dun's Review* (May 1966).
53. Ibid.
54. Ibid.
55. Ibid.
56. Byrne, John A. *The Whiz Kids*. New York: Currency Doubleday, 1993, p. 383.
57. "The Management of Litton Industries." *Dun's Review* (May 1966).
58. George Fenimore, interviewed by Bob

Wisehart, Sept. 1, 1998, transcript p. 22.

59. "What Puts the Whiz in Litton's Fast Growth." *Business Week* (April 16, 1966).

Chapter Four Sidebar

1. Self, Thomas M. "Litton Industries' Charles B. (Tex) Thornton." *The Executive* (Jan. 1980): 14.
2. "Litton: B-school for Conglomerates." *Business Week* (1967).
3. John Leonis, interviewed by Jeffrey L. Rodengen, June 26, 1998, transcript p. 35.

Chapter Five

1. O'Green, Fred. "Putting Technology to Work: The Story of Litton Industries." Speech to the Newcomen Society. Nov. 7, 1988.
2. Transcript of 1967 Litton Industries annual meeting.
3. Self, Thomas M. "Litton Industries' Charles B. (Tex) Thornton." *The Executive* (Jan. 1980): 14.
4. Den Knecht, interviewed by Jeffrey L. Rodengen, Jan. 14, 1999, transcript pp. 5–6.
5. Information provided by Glen McDaniel, Jan. 2000.
6. Lay, Beirne, Jr. *Someone Has to Make It Happen.* Prentice-Hall, p. 174.
7. Byrne, John A. *The Whiz Kids.* New York: Currency Doubleday, 1993, p. 486.

8. Rukeyser, William S. "Litton Down to Earth." *Fortune* (April 1968): pp. 183, 184.
9. George Fenimore, interviewed by Bob Wisehart, Aug. 1, 1998, transcript p. 19.
10. Information provided by John Preston, Nov. 1999.
11. "The Shattered Image of Litton Industries." *Forbes* (Dec. 1, 1969).
12. O'Green, Fred. "Putting Technology to Work: The Story of Litton Industries." Speech to the Newcomen Society. Nov. 7, 1988.
13. Litton Industries 1967, 1968, 1969 and 1979 annual reports.
14. Litton Industries 1967, 1969, 1973 and 1974 annual reports.
15. O'Green, Fred. "Putting Technology to Work: The Story of Litton Industries." Speech to the Newcomen Society. Nov. 7, 1988.
16. Litton Industries 1970 Annual Report.
17. Gerald St. Pé, interviewed by Melody Maysonet, July 8, 1999, transcript 18.
18. "The Shattered Image of Litton Industries." *Forbes* (Dec. 1, 1969).

Chapter Five Sidebar

1. Switzer, George S. "Questing for Gems." *National Geographic* (Dec. 1971): 858.
2. Donald Lepore, interviewed by Melody Maysonet, July 23, 1999, transcript p. 26.

3. Ibid.
4. Barne, Valerie. *Newark Evening News* (Nov. 5, 1969): pp. 1, 4.
5. Donald Lepore, interviewed by Melody Maysonet, July 23, 1999, transcript p. 34.
6. Switzer, George S. "Questing for Gems." *National Geographic* (Dec. 1971): pp. 857–858.
7. Donald Lepore, interviewed by Melody Maysonet, July 23, 1999, transcript p. 24.

Chapter Six

1. O'Hanlon, Thomas, "A Rejuvenated Litton Is Once Again off to the Races." *Fortune* (Oct. 8, 1979).
2. Tindall, George B. and David E. Shi. *America.* 2nd ed. New York: W. W. Norton & Company, 1989, pp. 911–912.
3. Ibid.
4. Ibid.
5. "Inflation and Deflation." Microsoft Encarta 97 Encyclopedia.
6. Information provided by Glen McDaniel, Jan. 2000.
7. Information provided by Allan R. Baron, Advanced Technology group, Litton Industries, Sept. 3, 1999.
8. Katter, Una Vere. "Litton Data Systems: Command and Control Developer and Integrator," Data Systems Division internal publication, p. 5.
9. Information provided by Allen J. Bernardini,

Winchester and VEAM divisions.

10. Frank Tullis, interviewed by Melody Maysonet, Aug. 4, 1999, transcript p. 29.

11. Litton Industries 1973 Annual Report.

12. Katter, Una Vere. "Litton Data Systems: Command and Control Developer and Integrator," Data Systems Division internal publication, p. 4.

13. Litton Industries 1973 Annual Report.

14. Ibid.

15. Ibid.

16. Information provided by Allen J. Bernardini, Winchester and VEAM divisions.

17. Information provided by Dr. Richard True, Electron Devices Division, Oct. 28, 1999.

18. Litton Industries 1973 Annual Report.

19. Ibid.

20. Ibid.

21. Ibid.

22. "The Model Conglomerate Tries to Be an Operating Company." Business Week (Dec. 1, 1973): p. 70.

23. Ibid., p. 69.

24. O'Hanlon, Thomas. "A Rejuvenated Litton Is Once Again off to the Races." Fortune (Oct. 8, 1979).

25. Nancy Gaymon, interviewed by Jeffrey L. Rodengen, June 26, 1998, transcript p. 9.

26. Robert Knapp, interviewed by Pat Prince Rose, May 18, 1998, transcript p. 27.

27. O'Green, Fred. "Putting Technology to Work: The Story of Litton Industries." Speech to the Newcomen Society. Nov. 7, 1988.

28. Ibid.

29. Litton Industries 1973 Annual Report.

30. Litton Industries 1974 Annual Report.

31. Glen McDaniel, interviewed by Bob Wisehart, Aug. 17, 1998, transcript p. 48.

32. Self, Thomas M. "Litton Industries' Charles B. 'Tex' Thornton." The Executive (Jan. 1980).

33. Ibid.

34. O'Hanlon, Thomas. "A Rejuvenated Litton Is Once Again off to the Races." Fortune (Oct. 8, 1979).

35. Ibid.

36. Self, Thomas M. "Litton Industries' Charles B. 'Tex' Thornton." The Executive (Jan. 1980).

37. Information provided by Richard Hopman, LITEF division, Sept. 29, 1999.

38. Hessman, James D. "DD 963: On the Ways, and on the Way." Sea Power (May 1975).

39. John Preston, interviewed by Jeffrey L. Rodengen, June 26, 1998, transcript p. 2.

40. Hessman, James D. "DD 963: On the Ways, and on the Way." Sea Power (May 1975).

41. Ibid.

42. Ibid.

43. Glen McDaniel, interviewed by Bob

Wisehart, Aug. 17, 1998, transcript p. 43.

44. Ibid.

45. Remarks by Glen McDaniel at a Litton dinner honoring Robert H. Lentz. Bel Air Hotel, Los Angeles, Dec. 3, 1997.

46. Ibid.

47. Ibid.

48. Glen McDaniel, interviewed by Bob Wisehart, Aug. 17, 1998, transcript p. 47.

49. O'Hanlon, Thomas. "A Rejuvenated Litton Is Once Again off to the Races." Fortune (Oct. 8, 1979).

50. Donald Lepore, interviewed by Melody Maysonet, July 22, 1999, transcript pp. 6–8.

51. O'Hanlon, Thomas. "A Rejuvenated Litton Is Once Again off to the Races." Fortune (Oct. 8, 1979).

52. Ibid.

53. Litton Industries 1980 Annual Report.

Chapter Seven

1. Litton Industries 1984 Annual Report.

2. Tindall, George B. and David E. Shi. America. 2nd ed. New York: W. W. Norton & Company, 1989, pp. 930–947.

3. Litton Industries 1983 Annual Report.

4. Litton Industries 1981 Annual Report.

5. Lynn, Norm. "Litton's Milestone." Airline Executive (Nov. 1983).

6. Joseph Caligiuri, interviewed by Jeffrey L. Rodengen, April 9, 1999, transcript p. 11.

7. Information provided by Michael R. Worstell, Aero Products division, Sept. 13, 1999.

8. Ibid.

9. Knapp, Robert S. "The Laser Gyroscope." *New Scientist* (July 15, 1965): p. 149.

10. Joseph Caligiuri, interviewed by Jeffrey L. Rodengen, April 9, 1999, transcript pp. 11, 12.

11. Lynn, Norm. "Litton's Milestone." *Airline Executive* (Nov. 1983).

12. Litton Industries 1983 Annual Report.

13. Joseph Caligiuri, interviewed by Jeffrey L. Rodengen, April 9, 1999, transcript p. 34.

14. Litton Industries 1983 Annual Report.

15. Ibid.

16. Ibid.

17. Frank Tullis, interviewed by Melody Maysonet, Aug. 4, 1999, transcript p. 30.

18. Information provided by Richard George, Data Systems Division, Sept. 7, 1999.

19. Information provided by Dr. Richard True, Electron Devices Division, Oct. 28, 1999.

20. Litton Industries 1981 Annual Report.

21. Litton Industries 1982 Annual Report.

22. Information provided by Dr. Richard True, Electron Devices Division, Oct. 28, 1999.

23. Robert Del Boca, interviewed by Melody Maysonet, April 8, 1999, transcript p. 2.

24. Dave Wright, interviewed by Jeffrey L. Rodengen, Jan. 14, 1999, transcript p. 11.

25. Litton Industries 1983 Annual Report.

26. Ibid.

27. Den Knecht, interviewed by Jeffrey L. Rodengen, Jan. 14, 1998, transcript pp. 10–11.

28. "Defense Buildup Brightens Ingalls' Picture." *Jackson Clarion-Ledger* (March 11, 1984).

29. "Missile Cruiser Ticonderoga Joining Fleet." *Gannett News Service* (Jan. 16, 1983).

30. Litton Industries 1985 Annual Report.

31. "Defense Buildup Brightens Ingalls' Picture." *Jackson Clarion-Ledger* (March 11, 1984).

32. Information provided by Bob Lentz, Jan. 2000.

33. Ibid.

34. Litton Industries 1983 Annual Report.

35. Ibid.

36. Yergin, Daniel. *The Prize: The Epic Quest for Oil, Money & Power.* New York: Simon & Schuster, 1991, p. 237.

37. Litton Industries 1983 Annual Report.

38. Ibid.

39. Litton Industries 1987 Annual Report.

40. Litton Industries 1988 Annual Report.

41. Litton Industries 1983 Annual Report.

42. Ibid.

43. Ibid.

44. Litton Industries 1988 Annual Report.

45. Dr. David Miller, interviewed by Melody Maysonet, Nov. 11, 1999, transcript p. 6.

46. Litton Industries 1981 Annual Report.

47. Litton Industries 1983 Annual Report.

48. "Engulfed by Litton Industries." *The Economist* (Jan. 29, 1983): p. 65.

49. Litton Industries 1982 Annual Report.

50. Litton Industries 1981 Annual Report.

51. Litton Industries 1988 Annual Report.

52. O'Green, Fred. "Putting Technology to Work: The Story of Litton Industries." Speech to the Newcomen Society. Nov. 7, 1988.

53. Ibid.

54. George Fenimore, interviewed by Bob Wisehart, Dec. 21, 1998.

55. George Fenimore, interviewed by Jeffrey L. Rodengen, April 9, 1999, transcript p. 43.

56. Litton Industries 1985 Annual Report.

57. "Heard on the Street," *Wall Street Journal* (April 24, 1984).

58. Ibid.

59. Ibid.

60. Litton Industries 1984 Annual Report.

61. Carson, Teresa and Stewart Toy. "Litton's Defense May Be Its Best Offense." *Business Week* (June 24, 1985).
62. Litton Industries 1988 Annual Report.
63. Ibid.
64. O'Green, Fred. "Putting Technology to Work: The Story of Litton Industries." Speech to the Newcomen Society. Nov. 7, 1988.
65. Ibid.

Chapter Seven Sidebar

1. Litton Industries 1983 Annual Report.
2. "Engulfed by Litton Industries." *The Economist* (Jan. 29, 1983): p. 65.
3. Litton Industries 1983 Annual Report.
4. Robert Knapp, interviewed by Bob Wisehart, May 28, 1998.

Chapter Eight

1. Litton Industries 1993 Annual Report.
2. Tindall, George B. and David E. Shi. *America.* 2nd ed. New York: W. W. Norton & Company, 1989, p. 1142.
3. Ibid., p. 1159.
4. "Litton Presses Ahead with Reorganization." *Flight International* (Sept. 22, 1993).
5. Ibid.
6. Ibid.
7. Litton Industries 1988 Annual Report.

8. Litton Industries 1989 Annual Report.
9. John Leonis, interviewed by Jeffrey L. Rodengen, June 26, 1998, transcript p. 13.
10. Ibid., p. 14.
11. Information provided by Allan R. Baron, Advanced Technology group, Sept. 3, 1999.
12. Tim Paulson, interviewed by Jeffrey L. Rodengen, Sept. 21, 1998, transcript p. 5.
13. Mike Gering, interviewed by Melody Maysonet, April 23, 1999, transcript p. 10.
14. John Leonis, interviewed by Jeffrey L. Rodengen, June 26, 1998, transcript p. 15.
15. Ibid., pp. 14–15.
16. Henry Bodurka, interviewed by David Patten, April 5, 1999, transcript p. 18.
17. Litton Industries 1989 Annual Report.
18. Litton Industries 1990 Annual Report.
19. John Leonis, interviewed by Jeffrey L. Rodengen, June 26, 1998, transcript p. 13.
20. Litton Industries 1990 Annual Report.
21. Litton Industries 1991 Annual Report.
22. Litton Industries 1989 Annual Report.
23. Litton Industries 1991 Annual Report.
24. Litton Industries archives.
25. Litton Industries 1990 Annual Report.

26. Ibid.
27. Litton Industries 1991 Annual Report.
28. Litton Industries 1989 Annual Report.
29. Information provided by John Preston, Litton Industries, Nov. 1999.
30. Kramer, L.D., interviewed by David Patten, April 9, 1999, transcript p. 4.
31. John Leonis, interviewed by Jeffrey L. Rodengen, June 26, 1998, transcript p. 37.
32. Larry Frame, interviewed by Jeffrey L. Rodengen, July 27, 1998, transcript pp. 5–6.
33. John Preston, interviewed by Jeffrey L. Rodengen, June 26, 1998, transcript pp. 13–14.
34. Litton Industries archives.
35. Michael Brown, interviewed by Jeffrey L. Rodengen, July 27, 1998, transcript p. 7.
36. Information provided by Michael R. Worstell, Aero Products division, Sept. 13, 1999.
37. Information provided by Richard George, Data Systems Division, Sept. 7, 1999.
38. Boatman, John. "Litton Goes on the EW Offensive." *Jane's Defence Weekly* (Nov. 6, 1993): p. 51.
39. Darwin Beckel, interviewed by Jeffrey L. Rodengen, Sept. 21, 1998, transcript pp. 29–30.
40. Litton Industries 1993 Annual Report.

41. Robert Knapp, interviewed by Bob Wisehart, May 28, 1998.

42. Litton Industries 1992 Annual Report.

43. "Litton: A Leader in International Markets." *The Khaleej Times* (Nov. 12, 1995).

44. "Our Strength Is in Shipbuilding," *Wall Street Corporate Reporter* (Aug. 12–18, 1996).

45. Information provided by Dr. Richard True, Electron Devices Division, Oct. 28, 1999.

46. Laur, Colonel Timothy M. and Steven L. Llanso. *Encyclopedia of Modern U.S. Military Weapons.* New York: Berkley Books, 1995, p. 244.

47. Tom Hutchings, interviewed by Melody Maysonet, July 8, 1999, transcript p. 37.

48. Ibid., pp. 33, 34.

49. Steve Mazzo, interviewed by David Patten, April 5, 1999, transcript pp. 7–8.

50. Frank Tullis, interviewed by Melody Maysonet, Aug. 4, 1999, transcript p. 15.

51. Information provided by Allan R. Baron, Advanced Technology group, Sept. 1, 1999.

52. Litton Industries archives.

53. "Litton: A Leader in International Markets." *The Khaleej Times* (Nov. 12, 1995).

54. Litton Industries 1991 Annual Report.

55. John Leonis, interviewed by Jeffrey L. Rodengen, June 26, 1998, transcript p. 19.

56. Ibid., pp. 17–18.

57. John Preston, interviewed by Jeffrey L. Rodengen, June 26, 1998, transcript p. 8.

58. Larry Ball, interviewed by David Patten, April 6, 1999, transcript p. 13.

59. Robert Knapp, interviewed by Pat Prince Rose, May 28, 1998.

60. Michael Brown, interviewed by Jeffrey L. Rodengen, July 27, 1998, transcript p. 10.

61. John Preston, interviewed by Jeffrey L. Rodengen, June 26, 1998, transcript p. 9.

62. Boatman, John. "Litton Goes on the EW Offensive." *Jane's Defence Weekly* (Nov. 6, 1993): p. 51.

63. Litton Industries 1993 Annual Report.

64. Glen McDaniel, interviewed by Bob Wisehart, Aug. 17, 1998, transcript p. 48.

65. Litton Industries 1993 Annual Report.

66. Ibid.

67. Ibid.

68. Ibid.

69. Litton Industries archives.

70. Litton Industries 1993 Annual Report.

71. Ibid.

72. Donald Lepore, interviewed by Melody Maysonet, July 23, 1999, transcript pp. 21–22.

73. Litton Industries 1993 Annual Report.

74. John Leonis, interviewed by Jeffrey L. Rodengen, June 26, 1998.

75. Boatman, John. "Litton goes on the EW Offensive." *Jane's Defence Weekly* (Nov. 6, 1993).

76. "Litton Moves Its Headquarters out of Beverly Hills." *Los Angeles Business Journal* (Jan. 9, 1995).

77. Nancy Gaymon, interviewed by Jeffrey L. Rodengen, June 26, 1998, transcript p. 6.

78. Ibid., p. 5.

79. John Preston, interviewed by Jeffrey L. Rodengen, June 26, 1998, transcript p. 6.

Chapter Nine

1. John Leonis, interviewed by Jeffrey L. Rodengen, June 26, 1998, transcript p. 17.

2. Litton Industries 1995 Annual Report.

3. Litton Industries 1994 Annual Report.

4. Darwin Beckel, interviewed by Jeffrey L. Rodengen, Sept. 21, 1998, transcript p. 27.

5. George Fenimore, interviewed by Jeffrey L. Rodengen, April 9, 1999, transcript p. 5.

6. John Leonis, interviewed by Jeffrey L. Rodengen, June 26, 1998, transcript p. 30.

7. Tom Hutchings, interviewed by Melody Maysonet, July 8, 1999, transcript pp. 2, 3.

8. Jim Frey, interviewed by Jeffrey L. Rodengen, Sept. 21, 1998, transcript p. 14.

9. Nancy Gaymon, interviewed by the author, June 26, 1998.

10. Allen J. Bernardini, interviewed by David Patten, April 6, 1999, transcript p. 6.

11. Henry Bodurka, interviewed by David Patten, April 5, 1999, transcript p. 13.

12. Gerald St. Pé, interviewed by Melody Maysonet, July 8, 1999, transcript p. 6.

13. Katter, Una Vere. "Litton Data Systems Command and Control Developer and Integrator." Data Systems Division internal publication, pp. 1–6.

14. Ibid., p. 5.

15. Tom Hutchings, interviewed by Melody Maysonet, July 8, 1999, transcript p. 23.

16. Frank Tullis, interviewed by Melody Maysonet, Aug. 4, 1999, transcript p. 5.

17. Ibid., p. 7.

18. Tom Hutchings, interviewed by Melody Maysonet, July 8, 1999, transcript p. 25.

19. Litton Industries 1997 Annual Report.

20. Frank Tullis, interviewed by Melody Maysonet, Aug. 4, 1999, transcript p. 27.

21. Ibid., p. 5.

22. Katter, Una Vere. "Litton Data Systems Command and Control Developer and Integrator." Data Systems Division internal publication, p. 3.

23. Leonard Pomata, interviewed by Melody Maysonet, April 22, 1999, transcript pp. 5–6.

24. Litton Industries 1998 Annual Report.

25. Leonard Pomata, interviewed by Melody Maysonet, April 22, 1999, transcript p. 8.

26. Alden Munson, interviewed by Jeffrey L. Rodengen, July 27, 1998.

27. Financial Overview, Litton Industries, June 8, 1999.

28. "PRC Shines as a Strategic Piece in Litton's Business Arsenal." *Washington Post* (Dec. 26, 1995).

29. Alden Munson, interviewed by Jeffrey L. Rodengen, July 27, 1999, transcript p. 2.

30. Litton Industries 1997 Annual Report.

31. Litton Industries 1995 Annual Report.

32. Ibid.

33. Den Knecht, interviewed by Jeffrey L. Rodengen, January 14, 1999.

34. Litton Industries 1997 Annual Report.

35. Ibid.

36. Den Knecht, interviewed by Jeffrey L. Rodengen, Jan. 14, 1999, transcript p. 14.

37. Information provided by Michael R. Worstell, Aero Products division, Sept. 13, 1999.

38. Larry Frame, interviewed by Jeffrey L. Rodengen, July 27, 1998, transcript p. 5.

39. Ibid.

40. Litton Industries 1995 Annual Report.

41. Tom Hutchings, interviewed by Melody Maysonet, July 8, 1999, transcript p. 45.

42. Litton Industries 1996 Annual Report.

43. Tom Hutchings, interviewed by Melody Maysonet, July 8, 1999, transcript p. 44.

44. Ibid., pp. 49, 50.

45. Information provided by Michael R. Worstell, Aero Products division, Sept. 13, 1999.

46. Ibid.

47. Tom Hutchings, interviewed by Melody Maysonet, July 8, 1999, transcript pp. 46, 48.

48. "Litton: A Leader in International Markets." *The Khaleej Times* (Nov. 12, 1995).

49. Ibid.

50. Litton Industries 1994 Annual Report.

51. Litton Industries 1998 Annual Report.

52. Litton Industries 1997 Annual Report.

53. Litton Industries 1998 Annual Report.

54. Ibid.

55. Information provided by Piero Biagetti, Litton Italia division, Oct. 15, 1999.

56. Tom Hutchings, interviewed by Melody Maysonet, July 8, 1999, transcript p. 50.

57. Litton Industries 1998 Annual Report.
58. Frank Marshall, Jr., interviewed by Jeffrey L. Rodengen, Sept. 21, 1998, transcript p. 16.
59. "The Litton Post–Cold War Model President and CEO John Leonis Steers a U.S. Defence Corporation Upward." *NATO's Sixteen Nations* (No. 3/4, 1994).
60. Pasztor, Andy. "Avondale Says It Is Ready to Take $529 Million Offer from Litton." *Wall Street Journal* (June 2, 1999): p. A4.
61. Litton Industries 1997 Annual Report.
62. "Litton: A Leader in International Markets." *Khaleej Times* (Nov. 12, 1996).
63. Litton Industries 1994 Annual Report.

Chapter Nine Sidebar

1. *Bloomberg Business News* (March 18, 1996).
2. "Wall Street Ignores Litton's Quiet Growth, Diversification." *Defense News* (April 22–28, 1996).
3. Litton Industries 1996 Annual Report.
4. "Litton Plans to Continue Acquisition Spree," *Le Bourget Today* (June 17, 1997).
5. "Our Strength Is in Shipbuilding." *Wall Street Corporate Reporter* (August 12–18, 1996).

Chapter Ten

1. Remarks by Michael Brown at the Corporate Advanced Engineering Symposium, Washington, D.C., May 27, 1999.
2. Litton Industries news release, Woodland Hills, CA, March 24, 1998.
3. Litton Industries 1998 Annual Report.
4. Litton Industries news release, Woodland Hills, CA, March 18, 1999.
5. Information provided by Joe Ailinger, TASC division, Sept. 2, 1999.
6. Litton Industries 1998 Annual Report.
7. Ibid.
8. Tom Hutchings, interviewed by Melody Maysonet, July 8, 1999, transcript p. 28.
9. Ibid., pp. 28–29.
10. Information provided by Richard George, Data Systems Division, Sept. 7, 1999.
11. Litton Industries 1998 Annual Report.
12. John Leonis, interviewed by Jeffrey L. Rodengen, June 26, 1998.
13. Remarks by Michael Brown at the Institutional Investors Conference, New York City, June 8, 1999.
14. Dr. David Miller, interviewed by Melody Maysonet, Nov. 19, 1999, transcript p. 2.
15. Litton Industries 1998 Annual Report.
16. Dr. David Miller, interviewed by Melody Maysonet, Nov. 19, 1999, transcript p. 2.
17. Ibid., pp. 6–7.
18. Tom Hutchings, interviewed by Melody Maysonet, July 8, 1999, transcript pp. 65, 66.
19. Ibid., p. 78.
20. Larry Ball, interviewed by David Patten, April 6, 1999, transcript pp. 8–9.
21. Ibid., p. 9.
22. Tom Hutchings, interviewed by Melody Maysonet, July 8, 1999, transcript p. 73.
23. Kelly Coffield, interviewed by David Patten, April 20, 1999, transcript p. 6.
24. Ibid., p. 8.
25. Ibid., p. 9.
26. Information provided by Bob Schutz, Advanced Circuitry and Inter-Pak Electronics divisions, Aug. 16, 1999.
27. Information provided by Allen J. Bernardini, Winchester and VEAM divisions.
28. Allen J. Bernardini, interviewed by David Patten, April 6, 1999, transcript p. 1.
29. Ibid.
30. Information provided by Allen J. Bernardini, Winchester and VEAM divisions.
31. Louis Tabor, interviewed by Melody Maysonet, March 26, 1999, transcript p. 2.
32. Information provided by Kitty Coleman, Litton Network Access Systems division, Sept. 7, 1999.

33. Financial Overview, Litton Industries, June 8, 1999.
34. Ibid.
35. Remarks by Michael Brown at the Corporate Advanced Engineering Symposium, Washington, D.C., May 27, 1999.
36. Jim Cox, interviewed by Jeffrey L. Rodengen, Jan. 14, 1999.
37. Litton Industries 1998 Annual Report.
38. Litton Industries news release, Woodland Hills, CA, March 9, 1999.
39. Ibid.
40. Ibid.
41. Wald, Matthew L. "U.S. Shipyard to Build 2 Large Passenger Vessels." *New York Times* (March 9, 1999).
42. Dave Wright, interviewed by Jeffrey L. Rodengen, Jan. 14, 1999, transcript pp. 17, 19.
43. Litton Industries news release, Woodland Hills, CA, March 9, 1999.
44. Gerald St. Pé, interviewed by Melody Maysonet, July 8, 1999, transcript p. 11.
45. Pasztor, Andy. "Avondale Says It Is Ready to Take $529 Million Offer from Litton." *Wall Street Journal* (June 2, 1999): p. A4.
46. Gerald St. Pé, interviewed by Melody Maysonet, July 8, 1999, transcript p. 3.
47. Ibid., pp. 2–3.
48. Harry Halamandaris, interviewed by Jeffrey L. Rodengen, July 27, 1998, transcript p. 5.

49. Robert Del Boca, interviewed by Melody Maysonet, April 8, 1999, transcript pp. 4–5.
50. Harry Halamandaris, interviewed by Jeffrey L. Rodengen, July 27, 1998, transcript pp. 5, 12.
51. Mike Gering, interviewed by Melody Maysonet, April 23, 1999, transcript p. 3.
52. Information provided by Allan R. Baron, Advanced Technology group, Sept. 3, 1999.
53. Litton Industries news release, Woodland Hills, CA, March 1, 1999.
54. Information provided by Allan R. Baron, Advanced Technology group, Sept. 3, 1999.
55. Steven Lambert, interviewed by Melody Maysonet, April 28, 1999, transcript pp. 2, 3.
56. Litton Industries 1998 Annual Report.
57. Tom Hutchings, interviewed by Melody Maysonet, July 8, 1999, transcript pp. 40, 43.
58. Ibid., pp. 52–53.
59. Information provided by Dr. Richard True, Electron Devices Division, Oct. 28, 1999.
60. True, Richard, "Winning Wars and Keeping the Peace with Litton EDD Products." Electron Devices Division internal publication.
61. Ibid.
62. Information provided by Dr. Richard True, Electron Devices Division, Oct. 28, 1999.

63. Tom Hutchings, interviewed by Melody Maysonet, July 8, 1999, transcript p. 61.
64. Ibid., pp. 57–58.
65. Litton Industries 1995 Annual Report.
66. Litton Industries 1997 Annual Report.
67. Tom Hutchings, interviewed by Melody Maysonet, July 8, 1998, transcript p. 58.
68. Litton Industries news release, Woodland Hills, CA, March 2, 1998.
69. Mike Gering, interviewed by Melody Maysonet, April 23, 1999, transcript p. 5.
70. Ibid.
71. Information provided by Allan R. Baron, Advanced Technology group , Sept. 3, 1999.
72. Ibid.
73. Tom Hutchings, interviewed by Melody Maysonet, July 8, 1999, transcript p. 55.
74. Ibid., pp. 13, 14.
75. Ibid., p. 7.
76. Gerald St. Pé, interviewed by Melody Maysonet, July 8, 1999, transcript p. 17.
77. Tom Hutchings, interviewed by Melody Maysonet, July 27, 1998, transcript p. 9.
78. Ibid., p. 7.
79. John Preston, interviewed by Jeffrey L. Rodengen, June 26, 1998, transcript p. 18.
80. John Leonis, interviewed by Jeffrey L. Rodengen, June 26, 1998, transcript p. 30.

81. Frank Tullis, interviewed by Melody Maysonet, Aug. 4, 1999, transcript p. 11.

82. Information provided by John Stewart, LITEF division, Sept. 6, 1999.

83. "The Litton Post–Cold War Model President and CEO John Leonis Steers a U.S. Defence Corporation Upward." *NATO's Sixteen Nations* (No. 3/4, 1994).

84. Nancy Gaymon, interviewed by Jeffrey L. Rodengen, June 26, 1998, transcript p. 10.

85. Tom Hutchings, interviewed by Melody Maysonet, July 27, 1999, transcript pp. 8, 9.

86. Remarks by Michael Brown at the Corporate Advanced Engineering Symposium, Washington, D.C., May 27, 1999.

87. Joseph Caligiuri, interviewed by Jeffrey L. Rodengen, April 9, 1999, transcript pp. 14, 57.

88. Tom Hutchings, interviewed by Melody Maysonet, July 8, 1999, transcript p. 10.

89. Remarks by Michael Brown at the Corporate Advanced Engineering Symposium, Washington, D.C., May 27, 1999.

90. Ibid.

91. Tom Hutchings, interviewed by Melody Maysonet, July 8, 1999, transcript pp. 11–12.

92. Ibid., pp. 12, 13.

93. Remarks by Michael Steuert at the Institutional Investors Conference, New York City, June 8, 1999.

94. Ibid.

95. Ibid.

96. Remarks by Michael Brown at the Institutional Investors Conference, New York City, June 8, 1999.

97. Michael Brown, interviewed by Jeffrey L. Rodengen, July 27, 1998, transcript p. 6.

INDEX

1/2/01

MADISON COUNTY
CANTON PUBLIC LIBRARY SYSTEM
Canton, MS 39046